¡VIVA CHE!

contributions in tribute to
Ernesto 'Che' Guevara

edited by Marianne Alexandre

Lorrimer, London

First printing 1968

Manufactured in Great Britain by Villiers Publications Ltd,
London NW5

CONTENTS

ACKNOWLEDGEMENTS

We are especially grateful to the following people who contributed much time and effort to the project: Denise Alexandre, Jorge Bolaños, Alberto Korda, Osvaldo Salas and Cecil Woolf.

We would like to thank, for their help and suggestions, Téofilo Acosta, Ana Ortega Cáceres, Marysa Gerassi, Luis Korda, Vera Leech, Derek Lindsay, Ellen Maslow, Rafael Morante, Roberto Fernández Retamar, Guido Sanchez, Marie Schébéko, Daniel Schechter, Raúl Lazo Sotolongo, Jorge Timossi and Ed Victor.

Our thanks are also due to Casa de las Américas, the Cuban Embassy in London, Comision para perpetuar la memoria del Comandante Ernesto Guevara, Revista Cuba and Departamento de Prensa Extrangera (Ministerio de Relaciones Exteriores).

We would also like to thank, for the use of their photographs, Studio Korda, Keystone Agency, Magnum (John Hill in London), Osvaldo Salas, Comision Orientacíon Revolucionara and United Press International.

The piece by John Berger is reprinted by kind permission of *New Society*; the poem by Adrian Mitchell is reprinted by kind permission of *Peace News*; the piece by *OZ Magazine* is reprinted by kind permission of the editors; the song by Alasdair Clayre is included by kind permission of Albermarle Music, Ltd.

Other people have kindly helped us in many ways too various to specify. To all of these, our grateful thanks. Finally, we wish to thank all those who wrote in or sent contributions that we were unable to publish for lack of space.

MASA

At the end of the battle, when the fighter was dead,
A man came up to him and said:
' Do not die. I love you so.'
But, alas, the body stayed dead.

Two men came near him and repeated:
' Don't leave us. Be brave. Come back.'
But, alas, the body stayed dead.

Then twenty, a hundred, a thousand,
Five hundred thousand came and begged,
' Can so much love do nothing against death? '
But, alas, the body stayed dead.

Then millions came up; he was surrounded.
And all of them called: ' Brother, don't leave us. . . .'
But, alas, the body stayed dead.

Then all the men on earth came round.
The sad body saw them and was moved;
Slowly, he rose and kissed the first one,
And then began to walk. . . .

CESAR VALLEJO (Peru)
(1895-1939)

NOTES ON THE LIFE OF
ERNESTO 'CHE' GUEVARA

*Ernesto Guevara de la Serna was born in Rosario, Argentina, on
June 14th, 1928. His parents were Ernesto Guevara Lynch, civil
engineer of Irish descent, and Celia de la Serna, of Spanish
descent. It was a middle-class family with strong left-wing and liberal
tendencies. The Guevaras were free-thinkers, admirers of José Martí,
and on the side of the Republicans during the Spanish Civil War.*

*Ernesto was the eldest of five children; after him came Celia,
Roberto, Ana Maria and Juan Martin, in that order.*

JOSE AGUILAR: In 1937, my family fled from Spain to Argentina
where, at Alta Gracia, a city in the province of Córdoba, we met the
Guevaras. All the children became friends and played together every
day, really almost living together. The Guevara children were very
brave at games and sports, and we were a bit frightened of them.
Ernesto liked rough games very much; I remember one of his brothers,
Roberto, telling me how Ernesto would jump across three feet of
space from the third floor of their house to the next, just for kicks,
and then make fun of the other children because they did not dare
do the same thing.

In those days, our favourite writers were Jules Verne and Alexandre
Dumas.

Later, when Ernesto started high school in the city of Córdoba,
he studied English; but he always liked French better. He studied
French with his mother and liked to read French poetry. He was
also extremely fond of Pablo Neruda's poems, and would spend days
reciting some of them aloud.

My father, who was a doctor, was upset by the fact that Ernesto
read the works of Freud at the age of fourteen and that his parents
did not mind.

FERNANDO BARRAL: I met Ernesto in 1940. He was already incredibly
sure of himself and totally independent in his opinions. He was very
dynamic, restless, and unconventional. I think I secretly envied him
for his energy, his self-confidence and his boldness; the most striking
thing about him was his absolute fearlessness. The way he played
rugby also impressed us, and what made him so different from the
rest of us was that he seemed much more ' tough '.

ALBERTO GRANADOS: I met Ernesto in 1941 when he was at high

11

school with my brother Thomas. I was at University at the time. We Córdoba students, along with students from other universities, had gone on strike against the abuses committed on the university campuses. That was the reason I was arrested and taken to Córdoba central police commissariat. Rather than arrested, I should say kidnapped, for we were not tried. At that time my brother Thomas used to bring me food in jail, as they didn't feed us. One day, Ernesto, his school friend, came along. I spoke with the two of them and explained that the high school students should demonstrate in the streets so that people would know how we were being treated. What amazed me was young Ernesto Guevara's reaction to my proposal. He answered, 'Nothing doing, Alberto. Go out onto the streets so that the police can hit us with their clubs? Nothing doing. I'll go and demonstrate only if you give me a gun.'

CHE : At fifteen, a man already knows what he wants to die for, and he is not afraid of giving his life if he has found an ideal which makes this sacrifice easy.

ALBERTO GRANADOS : In spite of the asthma he suffered from all his life, Ernesto was a sports enthusiast, something we had in common; an education which alternated between Baudelaire's poetry and sports forged him spiritually and made him physically fit. From then on, he became involved with travel and action. He was at high school and I was at university; but as he enjoyed our company and as we were impressed by his intelligence and the depth of his knowledge, we became great friends. I used his father's library a lot. Ernesto was the main reader, and I came second. Without a doubt, he had an intellectual sense which, from childhood, enabled him to distinguish himself in all aspects of life. He enjoyed going out with us on trips to the country, learning many things that were later useful to us on our motorcycle trip across the continent. Years later, those experiences were necessary to him as a guerrilla. He learned how to set up a tent with few resources. We learned all of those things without ever thinking of future possibilities : it was just a healthy outdoor way of life that allowed us to get away a little from the ordinary routine of the student and city-dweller.

In 1946, Ernesto Guevara finished high school and the Guevara family moved to Buenos Aires. There, Ernesto began his medical studies.

ALBERTO GRANADOS : We all thought that, because of his knowledge of and facility in mathematics, he would study engineering. We were surprised when he told us he had enrolled in medical school. He had a part-time job in the city government and also did some voluntary work in an institute for Allergy Research.

When Ernesto was eighteen years old, he registered for compulsory military service, in accordance with Argentinian law. He was examined by a board of military doctors who, because of his asthma, pronounced him unfit for military service of any sort.

During all his holidays, Ernesto would travel by whatever form of transport was available to him. He sometimes went on foot, and at other times used a bicycle which had a small motor on it. In this manner, he travelled round the various provinces of Argentina: Tucumán, Mendoza, Salta, Jujuy and La Rioja. On another occasion, he signed up as crew member of a merchant marine ship and went to the Carribean. It was his first trip abroad.

CHE : I must admit that I have never felt like a foreigner anywhere, neither in Cuba nor in any of the countries I have been to; I felt Guatemalan in Guatemala, Mexican in Mexico, Peruvian in Peru. Just as I feel Cuban in Cuba today and, of course, Argentinian too, here and everywhere else.

ALBERTO GRANADOS : He used to say to his fellow students, ' While you stay here preparing for three exams, I plan to cover the province of Santa Fé, northern Córdoba, eastern Mendoza, and along the way study to pass those courses right along with you.' And, of course, he did just that and maybe more. He covered the route he had planned and passed his courses on top of it. He wasn't concerned about his grades, he was more interested in studying what would be useful to him and not what was good for getting high marks. . . .

Touring Latin America, becoming acquainted with its beautiful sights and the misery in which its inhabitants lived, was a long cherished dream. On those nights that I spent in the company of Guevara and my brothers in some mountain zone on a weekend or an excursion, our conversation was full of our future trip.

On December 29th, 1951, Ernesto set off with Alberto Granados for a long trip across Latin America by motorcycle. They planned to visit the whole length of the Pacific coast.

ALBERTO GRANADOS : If the motorcycle had held up, the trip would certainly not have turned out to be such a valuable and rewarding personal experience as it did. But the rickety motorcycle didn't make it. Shortly before we got to Santiago, Chile, when we still had not covered even an eighth part of our projected journey, the vehicle simply refused to go any further, and we mournfully wrapped it up in our pup-tent and left it in an out-of-the-way spot while we continued

13

our voyage on foot. This change gave us an opportunity to know the people. We had to get various odd jobs to earn enough money to continue on our trip. We worked as truck drivers, porters, seamen, cops and doctors and dishwashers. Trudging along without a cent in our pockets, we arrived at the gates of the ' Braden Company ' mine at Chuquicamata, Chile. Certainly, Braden and his cohorts never dreamed that in early 1952 the guard who was then sleeping in their sentry box with his feet resting on a pair of military boots was none other than the man who was later to make Yankee imperialism shiver in *its* boots : Major Ernesto Che Guevara.

The two young men reached Peru. They were appalled by the condition of the Indians now totally degraded by hunger, exploitation and addiction to coca.

ALBERTO GRANADOS : I remember one day at Macchu Pichu where we stayed for several days. I was reclining on the ' sacrificial stone ' among the ruins; Che was sitting next to me, preparing a hot drink. I was speaking about creating a workers' community in the Andes and then winning over the government to make a revolution for these poor people who receive so few of the benefits of civilization. Ernesto smiled and said, ' Make the revolution without firing a shot? Are you crazy? '

Guevara and Granados travelled by boat from the port of Pucalpa along the Ucayali River, which is a tributary of the Amazon. After a stay at Iquitos, they travelled on to San Pablo where they stayed at a leprosarium, working in the laboratory and living with the lepers, playing basketball with the patients, taking them on excursions and doing all they could to help.

When the time came to leave, Guevara and Granados decided to cross the Amazon and reach Leticia in Colombia, where the Amazon arrives at the intersection of three countries, Brazil, Peru and Colombia. The lepers built them a raft called the ' Mambo-Tango ' and organised a going-away party for the two young doctors.

ALBERTO GRANADOS : There, despite a heavy drizzle, was a boat packed with patients : men, women and children. When we arrived they cheered us and immediately began to sing. Everyone else had already gathered there and the band was naturally there too, saxophone in the lead, carrying on a musical dialogue with the patients. Then came the speeches. First three of the patients spoke, simply, awkwardly, but affectionately, expressing admiration for our voyage. When the third patient finished, it was my turn to speak. I was very moved, so my speech was not very good. . . . When the applause ended, they sang a farewell song and began to leave slowly and silently. The most moving part of the ceremony was to see the white boat slowly slipping away in the mist and the rain while the song of the chorus still reached us. It seemed dreamlike; everything was embellished by the affection and sense of brotherhood that we all felt in that moment.

They had many adventures and difficulties, for they missed Leticia and drifted further down river. When they made their way back to Leticia, they worked as soccer coaches, then got arrested in Bogotá. Finally, they reached Venezuela. Granados decided to stay and work at a leprosarium in Caracas and Ernesto met a family friend who owned a plane for transporting race-horses. This plane was returning to Buenos Aires via Miami; so Ernesto set off for Miami.

ALBERTO GRANADOS: Che told us that he had a hard time in Miami, that he went a lot to the library, that at first he had only a cup of coffee and milk during the day, that he became friendly with the owner of a cafeteria who gave him some food — until one day a Puerto Rican came in and began talking against the Truman administration. He was overheard by an FBI agent, and it was the same old story. Che had to make himself scarce.

Ernesto finally got back to Buenos Aires and continued his studies. He received his MD in March, 1953.

JOSE AGUILAR: He finished his student's career in a meteoric fashion, not terribly well, without getting brilliant marks, but extremely fast.

CHE: When I began my medical studies most of my ideals as a revolutionary did not exist. Like most other people, I longed for success. I dreamed of being a famous researcher and achieving something which might ultimately be of use to humanity. But due to a series of circumstances and also partly due to inclination, I began to travel all over America and got to know it well. Because of the conditions in which I travelled, I came into close contact with poverty and hunger and disease. Through lack of means, I discovered I was unable to cure sick children, and I saw the degradation of undernourishment and constant repression. In this way, I began to realise that there was another thing which was as important as being a famous researcher or making a great contribution to medical science: and that was to help those people.

JOSE AGUILAR: I noticed when he returned from that trip that he was much more interested in political issues. I heard him reading out a passage from his diary about Macchu Pichu. It was about the Spanish colonial domination which had taken over the Indian culture;

he described the Catholic churches he had seen which had been built over and had incorporated Inca remains.

After his graduation, Ernesto set out for Venezuela to visit Granados. With two or three companions he took a milk train that went from Buenos Aires to La Paz, a six-thousand mile trip. The train stopped at every city, large or small. He then crossed Lake Titicaca and went down to the coast to get to Venezuela. When he reached Guayaquil in Ecuador, he met Ricardo Rojo, an Argentinian lawyer in exile who had made a spectacular escape from prison, seeking asylum at the Guatemalan embassy in Buenos Aires. When Ernesto told Rojo that he was on his way to Caracas, Rojo replied: ' But Guevara, why do you want to go to Venezuela, a country that's good only for making money? Come with me to Guatemala where there's a real social revolution taking place.'

Granados received a note from Ernesto a few days later. It said, ' Petiso, I'm going to Guatemala. I'll write to you later.'

Ernesto Guevara arrived in Guatemala on December 24th, 1953. This was the beginning of ' El Che.' Because Argentinians use the monosyllable ' che ' to punctuate their conversation, Central Americans call anyone who comes from Argentina by this name.

CHE : To me, ' Che ' is the most important and most cherished part of my life. It means so much to me; everything that came before it, my surname and my Christian name, are minor, personal and insignificant details.

When Ernesto Guevara arrived in Guatemala, he wanted to go and practise as a doctor in the jungle. He made an application, but the Guatemalan authorities demanded that he renew his doctor's diploma first, which would have meant more years of study. Instead, he stayed in Guatemala City, leading a life on the margin of poverty, but full of social rewards. He met many young Latin American revolutionaries, including Hilda Gadea from Peru, who became his first wife.

DARIO LOPEZ : The first time I saw Che in Guatemala, he owned only one pair of worn-out shoes and always wore the same shirt that was never properly tucked into his trousers. I think he was heading for the hospital where he worked. Nico López pointed him out to me and said, ' Look, there's Che, the Argentine.' He was going through a very difficult period, and the only clothes he owned were the ones on his back. Occasionally, he would casually ask a pal, ' Could you lend me a pair of trousers or a shirt? ' (At times, the trousers were too big, but he didn't seem to mind.)

16

Nico López belonged to a group of young Cuban exiles who had participated in the assault on the Moncada and the Bayamo fortresses in Santiago de Cuba on July 26th, 1953. This assault had failed, but it had led to the formation of Fidel Castro's ' 26th of July' movement and in his departure for Mexico after his imprisonment.

HILDA GADEA : Nico López used to tell us all about what Fidel Castro had done. He admired Fidel, and it was during that period that many of us Latin American exiles began to respect Fidel. Nico would describe Fidel's discretion, the spirit of sacrifice with which he and his followers had attacked the Moncada fortress. Nico not only admired Fidel but also had tremendous faith in him.

In February, 1953, Jacobo Arbenz's left-wing régime had expropriated 225,000 uncultivated acres of arable land from the United Fruit Company owned by American investors.

CHE : The last American revolutionary democracy — that of Jacobo Arbenz — still in power in this area failed as a result of the cold premeditated aggression carried out by the USA, hiding behind the smokescreen of its continental propaganda. Its visible head was the Secretary of State, Dulles, a man who, through a rare coincidence, was also a stockholder and an attorney of the United Fruit Company. When the American invasion first took place, I tried to get together a group of young men like myself to fight back. In Guatemala, it was necessary to fight and almost nobody fought. It was necessary to resist, and almost nobody resisted.

HILDA GADEA: During the aggression, Che volunteered for guard duty while there was a black-out and the city was being bombed. He asked to go to the front, but he was never sent. Everyone knew he wanted to go and he finally had to take refuge in the Argentinian embassy. It was Guatemala which finally convinced him of the necessity for armed struggle and for taking the initiative against imperialism. By the time he left, he was sure of this.

MARIO DALMAU: Che had read the complete works of Marx and Lenin, and a whole pantheon of Marxist thinkers. His views were very lucid although, like all Argentinians, he liked to argue about them.

CHE: At that time, when I was in Arbenz's Guatemala, I had begun taking notes to try and assess what would be the duties of a revolutionary doctor. Then, after the United Fruit Company aggression, I realised one fundamental thing : to be a revolutionary doctor, you needed a revolution first.

In the summer of 1954, I slipped out of Guatemala into Mexico.

17

FBI agents were already arresting and killing off all those who might endanger the United Fruit Company government. In Mexico, I met up again with some militants of the 26th of July movement whom I had known in Guatemala. I also became friendly with Raúl Castro, Fidel's brother, and it was he who introduced me to the leader of the movement.

FIDEL CASTRO: Che was one of those people whom everybody liked on sight for his simplicity, his character, his naturalness, his sense of comradeship, his personality and his originality, even before finding out all the other fine qualities which distinguished him. His political formation had already attained a high degree of development. To convince a man of his type to join us did not need many arguments.

CHE: After my experiences travelling all over Latin America and after Guatemala, it would have taken very little to persuade me to join any revolution against a tyranny; but Fidel made a very great impression on me. He would confront the most impossible situations and resolve them. He was absolutely positive that if we set off for Cuba, we would get there. That once we got there, we would fight, and that by fighting we would win. His optimism was contagious. We had to act, to fight, to consolidate our position. To stop moaning and to start the real struggle. And in order to prove to the Cuban people that they could trust his word, he made his famous speech, ' In 1956, we shall be free men or martyrs ', announcing that, before the year was over, he would land somewhere in Cuba at the head of an expeditionary force.

Che began to train for guerrilla warfare in Mexico with the other young men who had decided to follow Fidel back to Cuba.

CHE: My almost immediate impression after attending the first few classes was that victory was possible, something I had doubted when I joined the rebel chief.

SONG FOR FIDEL by Che Guevara

Let's go,
Fiery prophet of the dawn,
Down winding secret paths,
To free the green land that you love.

Let's go,
To avenge many wrongs,
Our foreheads full of rebel stars,
Swearing to win or die.

18

When the first shot is heard and the land wakes up,
Like a girl startled out of sleep,
We'll be there by your side, calm warriors,
We'll be there.

When your voice proclaims to the four winds
Land reform, justice, bread and freedom,
We'll be there to echo your words,
We'll be there.

The day the wild beast is wounded in its side
By our liberating aim,
We'll be with you, hearts full of pride,
We'll be there.

Don't think that they can make us tremble,
Armed with gifts and decorations,
We want a rifle, bullets, a stick,
Nothing more.

And if their rifles mow us down,
We only ask for Cuban tears
As winding sheets for fighters
Washed away by the flow of history,
Nothing more.

On November 25th, 1956, the small yacht ' Granma ' set off for Cuba, with eighty-three men aboard. Their object was to liberate Cuba from the military dictatorship of Fulgencio Batista.

After a terrible journey, during which all the men aboard the ' Granma ' were racked with sea-sickness, they finally landed in Cuba, near Belic, a province of Oriente, and tried to head towards the Sierra Maestra mountain chain. Through inexperience, they got bogged down in a swamp and, after they emerged, they camped in a highly unsuitable spot in the sugar-cane fields. This place was known as Alegría de Pío.

MAJOR FAUSTINO PEREZ : At the mention of Alegría de Pío, the first thing that comes to my mind is the doctor who came with the ' Granma ' expedition. I'm thinking of Che in the grip of an asthma attack that never let up, while he never uttered a word of complaint. When we stopped to rest at Alegría de Pío, at a time when all of us, even the ones in perfect health, felt completely exhausted, Che devoted almost the entire day to caring for comrades whose feet had been cut to ribbons by the long walk.

But Fidel and his men had been spotted by Batista's army, which had closed in on the unsuspecting men and was now ready to attack.
CHE: At four o'clock that afternoon, without the slightest warning and to our complete surprise, we heard a shot, followed by a symphony of lead over our heads. In the kaleidoscopic scene, men ran by shouting, the wounded called for help, some men tried to take cover behind slender stalks of sugar-cane as if they were tree trunks, while others signalled in terror for silence by placing a finger over their lips amidst the roar of battle. . . . I personally felt the unpleasant sensation in my flesh of simultaneous baptism of fire and blood. We got out of there as best we could, every man for himself or in groups, not heeding our leader's orders, without contact with our captains and in a state of complete confusion. I remember the push that Major Almeida gave me since I did not wish to walk, and it was only thanks to his imperious orders that I got up and kept going, believing all the time that I was near death.

Of the eighty-two men who had set out with Fidel, only fifteen were left after the Alegría de Pío disaster. These fifteen wandered about in scattered groups through the cane-fields for nine days before finally meeting up again with their leader, Fidel.

When Fidel, who had only two men with him, joined up with the other twelve survivors of the 'Granma' expedition, he made his shortest speech: 'We have already won the war.'
CHE: It was incredible that this small group of men who did not know each other very well already spoke of victory and taking the initiative. But the one who had the greatest faith in the people, who at all times showed his extraordinary powers of leadership, was Fidel. Already, during those nights sitting under the trees anywhere, those long nights since our activities ceased at nightfall, we began to draw plan after plan for the present, for the near future, and for victory. The days passed, and, little by little, new recruits came in. The first peasants started joining us, some unarmed, some with weapons that had been left by our comrades in the homes of friendly people, or abandoned in the cane-fields as they fled.

FIDEL CASTRO: Then came our first victory and Che was already a soldier by then, as well as our doctor.

CHE: Our small troop already had twenty-two rifles at the time we stormed La Plata on January 17th, 1957, forty-five days after our

landing. We caught an Army Post of twelve to fifteen men by surprise, and they surrendered after an hour of fighting. Thus twelve new rifles were obtained from this action.

FIDEL CASTRO: By the time we had a second victory at El Uvero, May, 1957, Che was not only a soldier, but *the* most outstanding of that battle. He performed for the first time those amazing feats which became typical of everything he did.

CHE: The battle for the military detachment of El Uvero was the fiercest of the war; of the 120 to 140 men who took part, forty were put out of action, which meant that the dead and wounded amounted to approximately thirty per cent of the total combatants. The political outcome of the battle was extraordinary because it took place in one of the few moments—after the ' Granma ' invasion—when there was no press censorship in the island. The whole of Cuba spoke about El Uvero.

FIDEL CASTRO: On this occasion, Che distinguished himself not only as a fighter but as a doctor, helping both his wounded comrades and the enemy soldiers. As we had to leave El Uvero, hunted down by fresh enemy troops, someone had to stay behind with the wounded, and so Che remained. Helped by a small group of soldiers, he hid them, looked after them, saved their lives, and with them eventually joined up with our column once more.

CHE: In the early nomadic phase of guerrilla warfare, the guerrilla doctor must go everywhere with his comrades and fulfil all the other duties of a guerrilla as well, including that of combat. He must undertake the exhausting and sometimes heartbreaking task of looking after sick men without having in his possession the medicine that would enable him to save a man's life. During this stage, the doctor has the most influence on the other men and their morale, because, to a man in pain, a simple aspirin takes on importance if it is administered by someone who identifies with his suffering. During this phase, the doctor must identify completely with the ideals of the revolution, for his words will have more impact on the men than anybody else's.

When he returned with his little band of wounded to Fidel's column in July, 1957, Che was made leader of the second column to be formed in the Sierra Maestra.

CHE: A new column was being organised, with me as Captain. The column was made up of some thirty-five men, variously dressed and variously armed, but I was very proud of them. A few nights later I was to feel still prouder and closer to the Revolution, if that was possible, still more desirous of proving that my officer's insignia was deserved. We were writing a letter of greetings and appreciation to 'Carlos' — Frank País's clandestine name — which was signed by all the officers of the guerrilla army who knew how to write — many of the Sierra peasants did not know how to read or write, but they were part of the guerrillas. The signatures appeared in one column and, next to them in another column, the signer's rank. When my turn came to sign, Fidel said simply, 'Make it Major.' Thus, informally and almost off-handedly, I was promoted to Major of the Second Column of the Guerrilla Army, later known as Column No. 4. The trace of vanity that is within all of us made me feel the proudest man in the world that day. The symbol of my new rank, a small star, was given to me by Celia, together with one of the wrist-watches that had been ordered from Manzanillo. From that time on, we in the Second Column, much less harassed than the First headed by Fidel because of our lesser political importance, were able to form the bases of the first factories and more permanent camps, which would end our nomadic life. We carried through some actions of little importance, but the most important thing was precisely that stabilisation worked out with great difficulty by transporting materials from very distant regions on our shoulders.

RAFAEL CHAO : His black beret had a tiny gilt metal star on it. He could be seen, sometimes very late, sitting on his hammock and writing down his notes. He never took a rest without writing down some notes. He also liked discussion very much. When everyone was already asleep, he would take a walk through the camp, looking for someone who felt like having a talk.

ONIRIA GUTIERREZ, *the first woman member of Che's column, who joined up in August, 1957, when she was only eighteen*: On one occasion Che asked me about my religious beliefs. This led me to ask him if he himself was religious. 'No,' he answered, 'I can't be religious because I'm a communist.' I was dumbfounded; being so young, I had had no political education and had only ever been told terrible things about communists. So that I jumped up in my hammock and protested, 'No, you can't be a communist because you're such a good man.' This made Che laugh a great deal and he began explaining to me all the things I did not know.

On another occasion, we sat discussing in a group. There were some among us who always used to say that, once we had won against Batista, we would have to go and fight in other countries; it was while we were discussing this that I asked Che, 'Do you feel Argentinian, Che? How did you come to be here? I can understand why we're

26

here, but you . . .' He understood what I meant and answered me with his usual kindness. I will never forget what he said, ' It's because we all have to help one another.' I also remember him saying that he would not die of old age; he insisted on this point because, even then, I think he always meant to go on with the struggle.

CHE : We were able to put up a shoe factory and a saddlery, an armoury with its electric lathe, a tin works, and a smithy for the purpose, among other things, of filling small metal grenades to be fired from a gun — an invention of ours. It was fired with a blank cartridge and was dubbed ' M-26 '. We also built schools, recreation areas and ovens to bake bread. Later on, the Radio Rebelde transmitter was installed, and our first clandestine newspaper *El Cubano Libre* was published.

RICARDO MARTINEZ, *an announcer for Radio Rebelde* : I remember that Comandante Ernesto Che Guevara used to smoke a pipe on which were carved the names of places where he had fought. The pipe was covered with Sierra Maestra names, Alegría de Pío, La Plata, Palma Mocha, El Uvero, El Hombrito, Pino del Agua. . . .

El Che always drank maté, which is an Argentinian custom, and he took coffee without sugar. He carried a camera about with him, along with the gun which never left his side, and the equally vital inhaler which he used to overcome his attacks of asthma.

Often, he used to go about riding on a white mule.

On one occasion, when the Argentinian journalist, Jorge Ricardo Masetti, interviewed him on the Conrado Heights near the rebel radio station, enemy planes began to drop bombs on the area.

Instinctively, everyone dived for cover under the trees except for Che who refused to move. He insisted on continuing the interview with Masetti while the bombardment was going on. His reason was that the sound of gunfire and of bombs exploding which would be heard over the broadcast would prove to listeners that the criminal dictatorship cared nothing for the lives of the peasants in the area.

It was a bold reaction and we all felt ashamed of having taken cover; and so we left our hiding places and followed the example of Comandante Guevara who still sat there calmly carrying on with the interview.

A whole succession of victories now began for the guerrilla army which had effectively liberated a part of Cuban territory. In one victorious battle after another against Batista's army, the guerrillas were able to capture more and more arms, also recruiting more and more men both from the cities and the countryside. In March, 1958,

27

Major Raúl Castro, at the head of the Sixth Column, was able to go and form a Second Eastern Front in the north of the Oriente Province. By the summer of 1958, the guerrilla army felt strong enough to start moving west up the island towards Havana.

CHE: It was decided to initiate a march to Las Villas, the central province of Cuba. In the military order sent to us, the principal strategic plan indicated was to cut systematically the communications between the two extremities of the island. Further, I was ordered to establish relations with all the political groups that were in the mountain parts of that region and was given ample military powers to govern the zone under my charge.

It turned out to be an extremely difficult and arduous undertaking. Che's column had to march through unprotected and unfriendly territory, constantly harassed by Batista's army, without the cover of the Sierra hills nor the support of the Oriente population.

CHE: Those were days of fatiguing marches across desolate areas with nothing but mud and water. We were hungry, we were thirsty, and we could hardly move ahead; our legs felt like lead, and our weapons weighed us down. A mood of pessimism came creeping in. Hunger and thirst, fatigue, a feeling of helplessness in the face of the enemy, which was encircling us more and more, and above all, the terrible foot disease known in the country as *mazamorra* — which made each step taken by our soldiers intolerable torture — turned us into an army of ghosts. Day by day, the physical condition of our troop was deteriorating. We had food every other day, and not always then. The only way to keep the exhausted men going was by swearing at them, pleading with them, and yelling insults at them.

After a month and a half of marching, the exhausted troop finally reached the mountain range of Las Villas, ' that blue patch in the West' which filled Che's men with new hope when they first saw it in the distance.

CHE: Our first job when we arrived in the Sierra del Escambray was clearly defined: to harass the dictatorship's military apparatus, above all his communications. Our immediate objective was to prevent elections from being held. But work was made difficult by the short time left before the elections, which were scheduled for November 3rd. The days preceding November 3rd were ones of extraordinary activity: our columns mobilised in all directions, with the result that few voters in those areas cast ballots. Troops led by Camilo Cienfuegos in the northern part of the province paralysed the electoral farce. In general, everything from the transport of Batista soldiers to the movement of merchandise came to a halt. In the November and December of 1958, we gradually closed off the highways. The central railway line was cut at several points. And so the island was effectively divided. Nearly all communications between Havana and the cities east of Santa Clara were cut off.

Che's column was able to take and to hold many towns on the way to Santa Clara, the principal objective. Fomento, Cabaiguan, Guaios and Placetas all fell. On December 29th, 1958, Che and his men attacked Santa Clara, the focal point of the island's central plain, a city with a population of 150,000, which was the nerve centre of the nation's railways and communications. In spite of an armoured train rushed by Batista's army to the city, Santa Clara fell. This last campaign, brilliantly planned and fought by Che, helped finally to overthrow Batista's regime. It was just after the fall of Santa Clara that Batista fled Cuba. On January 2nd, 1959, Che Guevara and Camilo Cienfuegos entered Havana at the head of their columns.

CHE : I believe that the Cuban Revolution accomplished three radical alterations in the mechanism of Latin American revolutionary movements by demonstrating that :

1. The people's forces can win a war against the regular army;
2. It is not necessary to wait until all conditions are favourable to start a revolution; the insurrection itself can bring about those conditions;
3. In the underdeveloped nations of America, the basic field of action for armed struggle must be the countryside.

On February 9th, 1959, in consideration for services rendered to Cuba, Che Guevara was declared a full-fledged Cuban citizen by the Council of Ministers. On June 2nd, he married his comrade-in-arms, Aleida March, whom he had met during the revolutionary war. A few days later, he left for an extended tour of the Afro-Asian countries. This was to be the first of many such tours to the countries of the Third World and the socialist nations. Che acted as a representative of the Cuban Revolution and as head of various Cuban commercial delegations and missions. In the October of that year, he was made chief of the Industrial Department of the National Institute of Agrarian Reform.

CHE : Agrarian reform meant the destruction of monopolies which prevented the peasantry from working the land. It meant helping them to grow produce without the fear of getting into debt or being squeezed by the land-owners. From the start, the reform guaranteed to both farmers and agricultural workers the ownership of the land, the necessary technical aid of qualified personnel, and material and financial assistance. It eliminated the *latifundia* system which had consisted of paying rent with a part of the crop. It meant the full use and cultivation of arable lands which, under the capitalistic-mono-polistic system, had been deliberately allowed to remain fallow for economic reasons. It also tended towards the gradual elimination of the one-crop economics, sugar in the case of Cuba, which is the bane of underdeveloped countries.

On November 26th, 1959, the Council of Ministers appointed Che Guevara President of the National Bank of Cuba, in charge of the nation's finances. Many banknotes in Cuba still carry the signature: ' Che '.

IVAN ARGENTINSKI: My second meeting was in his office, as Governor of the National Bank. A very comfortably furnished room, left over from the past. Che Guevara met me like an old friend and said that he was entirely at my disposal. I started with a story which I had just heard :

After the victory, Fidel Castro called his nearest assistants and said :

' I want one of us to be Governor of the National Bank. Which one of you is an economist? '

' I ! ' Che said and raised his hand.

' Good, then you'll be Governor! But you're a doctor, aren't you? When did you turn economist? '

' Oh, I thought you asked which one of us was a communist ! '

Guevara laughed aloud, but neither confirmed nor denied the truth of the story.

At first he repeated several times that he liked cheerful people with a sense of humour and that he enjoyed funny stories, but he soon switched to a long and serious talk.

I. F. STONE : The word that first came to mind on meeting Che Guevara was simplicity. I had been waiting to see him for some time late at night in the Cuban National Bank building in Havana. He was the first man I had ever met whom I thought not just handsome but beautiful. With his curly reddish beard, he looked like a cross between a faun and a Sunday-school print of Jesus. Mischief, zest, compassion and a sense of mission flashed across his features during our interview. But what struck me most of all was that he seemed in no way changed, corrupted or intoxicated by the power which had suddenly fallen into his hands. He spoke with that utter sobriety which sometimes masks immense apocalyptic visions. The focus of his political

30

concern was not Moscow but his America — from the Mexican sierra to the Argentinian pampas — the America we forget when we ethno-centrically use the word in the United States. Of our talk on that first visit I remember the vivid relic of a fragile hope soon dissipated. ' We are going to be the Tito of the Carribean,' Che said of the Castro regime. ' You get along with Tito and you will gradually reconcile yourself to getting along with us.' But accommodation with a rebel from the Russian empire was quite different from accommo-dation with a rebel from the American empire. American policy soon demonstrated that Castro would have to be Krushchev's protégé if he were to survive our animosity. On my second visit, some weeks before the Bay of Pigs, there was no more talk of Titoism. Now Che spoke with enthusiasm of what he had seen in his grand tour of the Soviet bloc. What impressed him most was the reconstruction of North Korea and the quality of its industrial output — here was a tiny country resurrected from the ashes of American bombardment and invasion. Perhaps he saw this as a preview of Cuba's fate.

In February, 1961, the Ministry of Industry was established by the revolutionary government and Che Guevara was named Minister.

CHE : We cannot proclaim before the tomb of our martyrs that Cuba is independent economically. Cuba cannot be independent when just one ship prevented from leaving the United States can make a factory go out of work in Cuba; when one simple order from any of the monopolies can paralyse a work centre here. Cuba will be independent when it has developed its natural wealth and when it has ensured by treaties and by commerce with all the world that no unilateral action by any foreign power can prevent it from maintaining its level of production and from keeping its factories going at full rate.

At this time, Fernando Barral wondered if the Cuban Major ' Che ' Guevara could be his childhood friend, Ernesto. On enquiry, he received the following reply from Che: ' Dear Fernando, I know you were not sure of my identity but suspected that it was not me. In fact, it was not, because a lot of water has flowed under my bridge and nothing remains of the asthmatic individual you once knew, apart from the asthma. I hear you are married. I am too. I have two children, yet I remain an adventurer; only my adventures now have a truer purpose. This survivor from the past sends your family greetings, and for you a friendly embrace from Che, which is hence-forth my name.'

FERNANDO BARRAL : I saw him one evening at the Latino-Americano stadium where a Cuban team was playing against a Russian one. I

31

went over to him and we sat together for the remainder of the match, after which we set off for the Ministry. We went by car. He was driving and as we passed through the crowd, people called out, ' Che, Che ', catching him by the hand and trying to touch his clothes.

During the following years, Che dedicated himself as completely to the creation of a true economic and social revolution in Cuba as he had dedicated himself to the establishment of Castro's revolutionary régime. It was very hard work because, as he wrote, ' It is easy in moments of extreme peril to have recourse to moral incentives; but to maintain moral incentives at a high level at other times, new values have to be instilled into individual consciences. The whole of society has to be turned into a vast school. Underdevelopment on the one hand, and the withdrawal of capital to ' civilized ' countries on the other hand, make impossible a rapid transformation without any sacrifices. We still have a great deal to do before we can reach a satisfactory level of economic development, and the temptation to have recourse to the old methods, to go back to the system of material incentives as a means of economic development, is very great. *But Che Guevara was also convinced that this had to be avoided at all costs because,* ' for man fully to realise himself, the concept of man as commodity must cease to exist, and society must give him his share in exchange for the accomplishment of a social duty. Man can attain his full stature only when he can produce without the physical necessity of selling himself like a piece of merchandise.' *Che always maintained that material obligations had to be turned into moral ones, or else men would continue to remain alienated from society and from their own natures.* ' We must create a new man who is neither left over from the 19th Century nor a product of our own corrupt and decadent century. It is the 21st Century man we must create.'

The attempt to reconcile the practical necessities of Cuba's economy with the theoretical aspirations implicit in the Revolution occupied all Che's time. Every Sunday, he would leave for voluntary work in the fields or the factories. In 1964, he received a badge and a certificate for communist work for over 240 hours of voluntary production work in a six-month period. He also wrote many articles, letters and books including ' Memoirs of the Revolutionary War ', ' Guerrilla Warfare ' and ' Man and Socialism in Cuba ': in many speeches, he attempted to clarify the ideals that underlay his concepts.

CHE: ' If the revolutionary's ardour cools off once the most urgent tasks have been accomplished at the local scale, and if he forgets proletarian internationalism, the revolution itself ceases to be a force and settles back into a comfortable torpor which can be exploited by our irreconcilable enemies, the imperialists, who then gain ground.'

At some time during the Spring of 1965, Che Guevara disappeared from Cuba. Before he left he wrote several farewell letters.

To FIDEL: Other nations in the world call for my modest efforts. I can do what you are prevented from doing by your responsibilities in Cuba, and the hour has come to part . . .

. . . I say once again that I release Cuba from all responsibility except that of serving as my example. That if my final hour comes beneath other skies, my last thought will be for this people and especially for you. That I thank you for what you taught me and for your example, and that I will try to be true to my beliefs, whatever the final consequences. That I have always identified with the world outcome of our Revolution, and I am now following that path. That wherever I go, I will feel it is my duty to be a Cuban revolutionary, and to act as one. That I leave my wife and my children nothing, and I am not sorry, but glad it should be so. That I can do nothing for them as the State will give them enough to live on and will educate them.

I have many things to tell you and our people, but I feel they would be superfluous; words cannot express what I would wish to say. . . .

To HIS PARENTS: Once more I feel Rosinante's flanks between my heels and so take to the road again, carrying my shield on my arm.

I believe that armed struggle is the only solution for those who are fighting to free themselves, and I am acting according to my convictions. Many will call me an adventurer, and I am one — only of a different sort, the sort who gamble their lives to prove what they believe. This time, the end may come. I do not seek it, but it is a logical possibility. Should this be so, this is my last embrace.

And now, a willpower which I have polished with an artist's love will sustain my weak legs and tired lungs. I will do it. Remember this minor twentieth-century *condottiere* from time to time and receive a kiss from your rebellious prodigal son.

To ALBERTO GRANADOS: I don't know what to leave you as a remembrance. I force you, then, to spend a good long time in the sugar-cane. My roving house will have two legs once again, and my dreams will know no frontiers, at least until bullets speak. I expect you, sedentary gypsy, when the gunsmoke settles.

Many rumours were in circulation after the departure of Che Guevara: it was said that he had been killed during the uprising in the Dominican Republic; that he was fighting in the Congo, in Vietnam, in Venezuela, in Laos. . . . No official news of him came until April, 1967, when a message was sent by him to the Tricontinental Solidarity Organisation in Havana.

CHE : . . . In Latin America the armed struggle is going on in Guatemala, Colombia, Venezuela and Bolivia; the first uprisings are cropping up in Brazil. There are also some points of resistance which appear and then are extinguished. But almost all the countries of this continent are ready for a type of struggle that, in order to achieve victory, cannot be content with anything less than establishing a government of socialist tendencies. . . . César Montes and Yon Sosa raise up their flag in Guatemala; Fabio Vásquez and Marulanda in Colombia; Douglas Bravo in the western part of the country and Américo Martín in El Bachiller, both directing their respective Venezuelan fronts. New uprisings shall take place in these and other countries of our America, as it has already happened in Bolivia, and they shall continue to grow in the midst of all the hardships inherent to this dangerous profession of the modern revolutionary. Many shall perish, victims of their errors; others shall fall in the tough battle that is coming; new fighters and new leaders shall appear in the warmth of the revolutionary struggle. . . . We must take the war to every corner where the enemy happens to take it; to his home, to his places of entertainment; a total war. It is necessary to prevent him from having a moment of peace, a quiet moment outside his barracks or even inside; we must attack him wherever he may be; make him feel like a cornered beast wherever he may move. Then his moral fibre will begin to decline. He will become even more beastly, but we shall notice how the signs of decadence begin to appear. And let us develop a true proletarian internationalism, with international proletarian armies; the flag under which we fight would be the sacred cause of redeeming humanity. To die under the flag of Vietnam, of Venezuela, of Guatemala, of Laos, of Guinea, of Colombia, of Bolivia, of Brazil — to name only a few scenes of today's armed struggle — would be equally glorious and desirable for an American, an Asian, an African, even a European. Each drop of blood spilt by a man in any country under whose flag he was not born is an experience passed on to those who survive, to be added later to the liberation struggle of his own country. And each nation liberated is a phase won in the battle for the liberation of one's own country. The time has come to settle our disagreements and to put everything at the service of the struggle. . . . How close and brilliant the future would seem if two, three, many Vietnams flourished throughout the world with their share of deaths and their immense tragedies, their daily heroism and their repeated blows against imperialism, impelled to disperse its forces under the sudden attack and the increasing hatred of all peoples of the world!

. . . Wherever death may surprise us, let it be welcome, provided that this, our battle-cry, may have reached some receptive ear and another hand may be extended to wield our weapons and other men be ready to intone the funeral dirge with the staccato chant of the machine-gun and new battle-cries of war and victory.

Hasta la Victoria Siempre! Patria o Muerte, Venceremos!

On October 8th, 1967, in the region of Santa Cruz, Bolivia, a group of specially-trained Bolivian rangers were engaged in action against a unit of guerrillas, whom they had encircled. After a fierce battle, the rangers were able to capture the wounded guerrilla leader. He was taken to the nearby village of Higueras, where he was kept in a tiny school. After repeated attempts to interrogate him, he was shot through the heart towards noon of the following day. His corpse was strapped to the runners of a helicopter and taken to the nearby town of Vallegrande. There, it was exposed in a shack, where it was viewed by the local population, as well as journalists and photographers. It was announced to the world that this Bolivian guerrilla fighter, known as Ramón, was in fact Major Ernesto ' Che ' Guevara. When Che's brother arrived in Bolivia to identify the body, he was told that the corpse had been incinerated and the ashes scattered.

MARIANNE ALEXANDRE

CONTRIBUTIONS IN TRIBUTE TO
ERNESTO 'CHE' GUEVARA

The *baas* thinks
When it comes
Napalm tanks
Wire dum-dums
Shrapnel whips
Electric shocks
Booby traps
Will block us

The *baas* thinks
Flesh and blood
Sinew flanks
Black and red
Shall not stand
The war machine
The steel wind
The iron whine

Che, now our fingers are propellors
Cities burn where our minds were numb
Our arms are the barrels of mortars
Our heads are fused like a bomb

You have turned our tribes to brigades
We flow remorseless where rivers ran
Our loins are the seed of grenades
Our ribs are the armoury of man

After you, we will never yield
We have one thing to give you, a life
And the bullet shall break on our shield
And the vulture shall fall on our knife

The *baas* fears
When it comes
We'll wash our spears
In blood and bones
But Che knows
It comes soon . . .
The white night grows . . .
See the black moon!

J. A. (South Africa)

What I felt, as a human being, on hearing of Che's death, was influenced by the experience of some years in socialist countries of Eastern Europe. In the People's Poland, for instance, where flats may be got in reasonable time only by paying in dollars, where I have heard of prosperous Party members being bribed for a place in a sanatorium, and where everything stagnates, there is a good deal of noble talk, on all the media, about revolutionary heroes, and this — if nothing else — has killed my romanticism.

I have never been to Latin America, but I have read, in books by moderate writers, of a feudalism ranging from an outdated paternalism to a reign of terror. I have heard of wooden ploughs dodging round boulders on semi-barren hillsides and hunger allayed by manioc and bad coffee. In London I have mixed with irresponsible sons of the big landowners.

The revolution I really believe in is non-violent, but obviously to dictate non-violence to classes or races in a desperate plight is outrageously silly. I admire not only Che's courage and skill but his insistence that without a firm moral basis there can be no real revolution. Che's revolution won't triumph easily; his enemies have also studied his book and developed devastating tactics of counter-insurgency. But it will triumph in the end, and I hope for the emergence in Latin America of free, healthy, vivid societies without that canker of so many 'socialist' countries, a selfish élite of old ex-partisans and young technologists.

JOHN ADLARD (England)

TO THE MEMORY OF CHE

beneath the white map
or chaos
of the stars
the moon floats

he stands barefoot
on the cracked
warm earth
nightbirds shriek

swoop
his mineral sweat
makes luminous
his fear

he waits to kill
a tank
with an old gun
that his father

killed rabbits with
and a broken-
bladed knife
but no tank appears

so at dawn he turns
to go and two
soldiers
shoot him twice

walk away
not talking
buttoning
their pistol holsters

and when the sun
makes salt
from his sweat
and he lies dying

in the flat field
nursing his
torn belly
he tries to say

LYMAN ANDREWS (USA)

Here we are
appalled
outraged
even though this death is
one of the foreseeable absurdities

I'm ashamed to look at
the paintings
the armchairs
the carpets
to take a bottle out of the refrigerator
to tap out the three universal letters of your name
in the rigid machine
that never
never had
so pale a ribbon

Shame to feel the cold
and get near the stove as usual
to be hungry and eat
such a simple thing
to turn on the gramophone and listen in silence
to a Mozart quartet most of all

Shame on the comfort
shame on the asthma
when you comandante are falling
riddled
fabulous
brilliant
our conscience is full of holes

I hear that they burnt you
with what fire
are they going to burn the good
the glad tidings
the inexorable tenderness
that you brought with you and left behind
with your cough
and your earthenware cup
I hear that they burnt

all your vocation
minus a finger

enough to point out the way to us
and to accuse the monster who defiled you
and to tighten other fingers on the trigger

and so here we are
appalled
outraged

Sure that in time the leaden
amazement
will wear off
but the rage will remain
and its contours grow sharper

you are dead
you are living
you are falling
you are a cloud
you are the rain
you are a star

Where are you
if you are
if you are arriving
take off a moment at last
to breathe peacefully
to fill your lungs with sky

where are you
if you are
if you are arriving
it will be a pity if God does not exist

but there will be others
there are sure to be others
fit to welcome you
comandante.

Mario Benedetti (Uruguay)

On Tuesday, October 10th, 1967, a photograph (top photograph on page 104) was transmitted to the world to prove that Guevara had been killed the previous Sunday in a clash between two companies of the Bolivian army and a guerrilla force on the north side of the Rio Grande river near a jungle village called Higueras. (Later this village received the proclaimed reward for the capture of Guevara.) The photograph of the corpse was taken in a stable in the small town of Vallegrande. The body was placed on a stretcher and the stretcher was placed on top of a cement trough.

During the preceding two years 'Che' Guevara had become legendary. Nobody knew for certain where he was. There was no incontestable evidence of anyone having seen him. But his presence was constantly assumed and invoked. At the head of his last statement — sent from a guerrilla base ' somewhere in the world' to the Tricontinental Solidarity Organisation in Havana — he quoted a line from the 19th century revolutionary Cuban poet José Martí: ' Now is the time of the furnaces, and only light should be seen.' It was as though in his own declared light Guevara had become invisible and ubiquitous.

Now he is dead. The chances of his survival were in inverse ratio to the force of the legend. The legend had to be nailed. ' If,' said the *New York Times,* ' Ernesto Che Guevara was really killed in Bolivia, as now seems probable, a myth as well as a man has been laid to rest.'

We do not know the circumstances of his death. One can gain some idea of the mentality of those into whose hands he fell by their treatment of his body after his death. First they hid it. Then they displayed it. Then they buried it in an anonymous grave in an unknown place. Then they disinterred it. Then they burnt it. But before burning it, they cut off the fingers for later identification. This might suggest that they had serious doubts whether it was really Guevara whom they had killed. Equally it can suggest that they had no doubts, but feared his corpse. I tend to believe the latter.

The purpose of the radio photograph of October 10th was to put an end to a legend. Yet on many who saw it, its effect may have been very different. What is its meaning? What, precisely and unmysteriously, does the photograph mean now? I can but cautiously analyse it as regards myself.

There is a resemblance between the photograph and Rembrandt's painting of *The Anatomy Lesson of Professor Tulp.* The immaculately dressed Bolivian colonel has taken the professor's place. The two figures on his left stare at the cadaver with the same intense but impersonal interest as the two nearest doctors on the professor's left. It is true that there are more figures in the Rembrandt — as there were certainly more men, unphotographed, in the stable at Vallegrande. But the placing of the corpse in relation to the figures above it, and in the corpse the sense of global stillness — these are very similar.

Nor should this be surprising, for the function of the two pictures is similar: both are concerned with showing a corpse being formally and objectively examined. More than that, both are concerned with *making an example of the dead*: one for the advancement of medecine, the other as a political warning. Thousands of photographs are taken of the dead and the massacred. But the occasions are seldom formal ones of demonstration. Doctor Tulp is demonstrating the ligaments of the arm, and what he says applies to the normal arm of every man. The colonel is demonstrating the final fate — as decreed by ' divine providence ' — of a notorious guerrilla leader, and what he says is meant to apply to every guerrillero on the continent.

I was also reminded of another image : Mantegna's painting of the dead Christ, now in the Brera at Milan. The body is seen from the same height, but from the feet instead of from the side. The hands are in identical positions, the fingers curving in the same gesture. The drapery over the lower part of the body is creased and formed in the same manner as the blood-sodden, unbuttoned, olive-green trousers on Guevara. The head is raised at the same angle. The mouth is slack of expression in the same way. Christ's eyes have been shut, for there are two mourners beside him. Guevara's eyes are open, for there are no mourners : only the colonel, a US intelligence agent, a number of Bolivian soldiers and the thirty journalists. Once again, the similarity need not surprise. There are not so many ways of laying out the criminal dead.

Yet this time the similarity was more than gestural or functional. The emotions with which I came upon that photograph on the front page of the evening paper on that Wednesday afternoon were very close to what, with the help of historical imagination, I had previously assumed the reaction of a contemporary believer might have been to Mantegna's painting. The power of a photograph is comparatively short-lived. When I look at the photograph now, I can only reconstruct my first incoherent emotions. Guevara was no Christ. If I see the Mantegna again in Milan, I shall see in it the body of Guevara. But this is only because in certain rare cases the tragedy of a man's death completes and exemplifies the meaning of his whole life. I am acutely aware of that about Guevara, and certain painters were once aware of it about Christ. That is the degree of emotional correspondence.

The mistake of many commentators on Guevara's death has been to suppose that he represented only his military skill or a certain revolutionary strategy. Thus they talk of a setback or a defeat. I am in no position to assess the loss which Guevara's death may mean to the revolutionary movement of South America. But it is certain that Guevara represented and will represent more than the details of his plans. He represented a decision, a conclusion.

Guevara found the condition of the world as it is intolerable. It had only recently become so. Previously, the conditions under which two thirds of the people of the world lived were approximately the same as now. The degree of exploitation and enslavement was as great. The suffering involved was as intense and as widespread. The waste was as colossal. But it was not intolerable because the full measure of the truth about the condition was unknown — even by those who suffered it. Truths are not constantly evident in the circumstances to which they refer. They are born — sometimes late. This truth was born with the struggles and wars of national liberation. In the light of the newborn truth, the significance of imperialism changed. Its demands were seen to be different. Previously it had demanded cheap raw materials, exploited labour and a controlled world market. Today it demands a mankind that counts for nothing.

Guevara envisaged his own death in the revolutionary fight against this imperialism. ' Wherever death may surprise us, let it be welcome, provided that this, our battle-cry, may have reached some receptive ear and another hand may be extended to wield our weapons and other men be ready to intone the funeral dirge with the staccato chant of the machine-gun and new battle-cries of war and victory.'

His envisaged death offered him the measure of how intolerable his life would be if he accepted the intolerable condition of the world as it is. His envisaged death offered him the measure of the necessity of changing the world. It was by the licence granted by his envisaged death that he was able to live with the necessary pride that becomes a man.

At the news of Guevara's death, I heard someone say : ' He was the world symbol of the possibilities of one man.' Why is this true? Because he recognised what was intolerable for man and acted accordingly.

The measure by which Guevara had lived, suddenly became a unit which filled the world and obliterated his life. His envisaged death became actual. The photograph is about this actuality. The possibilities have gone. Instead there is blood, the smell of formol, the untended wound on the unwashed body, flies, the shambling trousers: the small private details of the body rendered in dying as public and impersonal and broken as a razed city.

Guevara died surrounded by his enemies. What they did to him while he was alive was probably consistent with what they did to him after he was dead. In his extremity he had nothing to support him but his own previous decisions. Thus the cycle was closed. It would be the vulgarest impertinence to claim any knowledge of his experience during that instant or that eternity. His lifeless body, as seen in the photograph, is the only report we have. But we are entitled to deduce the logic of what happens when the cycle closes. Truth flows in the obverse direction. His envisaged death is no more the measure of the necessity for changing the intolerable condition of the world. Aware now of his actual death, he finds in his life the measure of his justification, and the world-as-his-experience becomes tolerable to him.

The foreseeing of this final logic is part of what enables a man or a people to fight against overwhelming odds. It is part of the secret of the moral factor which counts as three to one against weapon power.

The photograph shows an instant: that instant at which Guevara's body, artificially preserved, has become a mere object of demonstration. In this lies its initial horror. But what is it intended to demonstrate? Such horror? No. It is to demonstrate, at the instant of horror, the identity of Guevara and, allegedly, the absurdity of revolution. Yet by virtue of this very purpose, the instant is transcended. The life of Guevara and the idea or fact of revolution immediately invoke processes which preceded that instant and which continue now. Hypothetically, the only way in which the purpose of those who arranged for and authorised the photograph could have been achieved, would have been to preserve artificially at that instant the whole state of the world as it was: to stop life. Only in such a way could the content of Guevara's living example have been denied. As it is, either the photograph means nothing because the spectator has no inkling of what is involved, or else its meaning denies or qualifies its demonstration.

I have compared it with two paintings, because paintings, before the invention of photography, are the only visual evidence we have of how people saw what they saw. But in its effect it is profoundly different from a painting. A painting, or a successful one at least, comes to terms with the processes invoked by its subject matter. It even suggests an attitude towards those processes. We can regard a painting as almost complete in itself.

In face of this photograph we must either dismiss it, or complete its meaning for ourselves. It is an image which, as much as any mute image ever can, calls for decision.

JOHN BERGER (England)

SPEAKING OF CHE

Now Che no longer lives, it's true,
Che has died, comrade repeat
but also repeat what I say with you :
that the enemy is trembling.

Let's sing, not for a fiesta,
but to prepare for the hard struggle ahead
every death must be paid for, comrades,
the enemy has to pay the price

Hard has been the luck
of this rich downtrodden continent
until the day the rifle flame
sets the land alight
and claims its just reward

That rifle won't fall silent for a minute
for if the firm hand
of Che has let go
another hand is sure to take it up.
Only the bullet matters
and the thought that directs its course.

We have bullets, we have rifles,
we have determined guerrillas,
they know where they are marching,

even in sorrow their hearts rejoice;
the enemy's luck will run out,
and his fate is to die in darkness

People will call out the names
of the enemies, of the ruthless officers,
of the Yankees with their war machines,
of the bosses who own the money and the wheels,
the plantations and the land.

And we, who are we?
We are all the poor and the beaten,
the humiliated but determined
poor but worthiest inhabitants
of this volcanic continent.

With Che we go through ragged valleys
through prairies and through cities.
We will carry on until
One day we set fire to the mountain

We're not complaining nor asking for anything
from our oppressors
we will never argue with them.
We will travel, comandante, along the bullet's path
and wander from one battle to the next.

And what are we fighting for,
and why so ready to make the sacrifice,
if not for the love of bread and fruits,
for the sweat of the common people,
for a dawn of American love
for a day of victory and socialism?

Che said in his guerrilla's language
death is a concept
which comes up a thousand times over
and victory is the myth
of the guerrilla's dreams;
in his deep hard sleep
he reckons on his dream

Tell me, comandante,
where are all the leaders
to go on with the fight?
and where are the future warriors?
Some are already struggling
others are being born among the leaves and by the rivers,
they are being nourished by their earth and their sky,
which are yours too, comandante, as well as mine.

Quickly, back into battle,
the fight must not ease up,
our weapons glitter redly,
as we go forward, burning with sacred hatred.

We will be worthy, comandante,
we swear it by the revolution!

SARANDY CABRERA (Uruguay)

Whatever I might try to write to express my admiration for Ernesto
Che Guevara, living or dead, seems unreal to me. I hear his laughter,
full of irony and commiseration answering me. I am here, sitting
in my study, surrounded by my books, in the false peace and the false
prosperity of Europe, and I devote a brief interval in my daily labours,
to write without any risk, about a man who wanted to take on himself all the risks, who had not accepted the pretence of a temporary
peace, a man who demanded of himself, as of others, the greatest
spirit of sacrifice, convinced that every hesitation to sacrifice today
would cost far greater sacrifice tomorrow. For us, Guevara is this call
to the ultimate seriousness of everything concerning the revolution
and the future of the world, this radical criticism of every gesture
which serves to appease our conscience.

In this sense he remains the centre of our discussions and our
thoughts, no less in death than in life. His is a presence which does not
demand from us facile approval nor formal acts of homage: this would
result in misunderstanding and minimising the extreme rigour of his
lesson. The ' code of Che ' demands much from men, no less in the
manner of the struggle than in the perspective of the society which

should be born out of the struggle. As against the courage and coherence needed to take a thought and a way of life to its ultimate conclusion, let us show ourselves first of all modest and sincere, aware of what the ' code of Che ' means — a total transformation not only of society but of human nature, starting from ourselves — and aware of what separates us from putting it into practice.

Guevara's discussion with all those surrounding him, the long discussion which was his short life — from discussion to action to discussion without ever abandoning the gun — will not be interrupted by death. It will always continue to grow. So for an occasional and unknown questioner as I was, with a group of guests one afternoon in 1964 in his office in the Ministry of Industry, meeting him could not remain a marginal episode. The discussions that matter are those that go on silently in the mind. In my mind, the discussions with Che have gone on all these years, and the more time has passed, the more he has been right. And now, having died setting in motion a struggle which cannot stop, he will ever continue to be more and more right.

ITALO CALVINO (Italy)

Two names, above all others, sum up the new age of South America: Ernesto ' Che ' Guevara and Camilo Torres Restrepo.*

Both were heroes and both were martyrs. Both dedicated themselves to the same cause : the liberation of their people. And when I speak of their ' people,' I mean the oppressed, the exploited, the poor and the hungry.

The same flame burned in their hearts and gave them a heroic calling. They knew very well that they could put their youth to the service of freedom and that is what they had to do.

They believed that a political system which does not help the masses must be overthrown, and that a more equitable government, better adapted to resolve the problem of poverty, must be established in its place.

In temporal terms, the Christian ideal is to serve the poor and the

---

* The revolutionary Colombian priest who was killed in action, fighting with the Colombian guerrillas on February 15th, 1966.

down-trodden. It is an inhuman and wretched thing to drag out a life devoid of hope, due to the fault of a social order which cannot resolve the basic needs of man. The people of Latin America are being crushed by the ruling oligarchies and imperialism. El Che and Father Camilo rebelled against imperialistic domination because it represents a threat both to individuals and to underdeveloped nations.

To die so that men will recover hope and start struggling to win real freedom is a Christian act. Both Che Guevara and Father Camilo gave their lives for a Christian ideal. Both stand for the ultimate expression of Justice, which is one of the fundamental tenets of Christianity.

I agree with Olivier Maillard when he claims that the fight for justice, the sacrifice of one's life for one's brothers, the generosity of an undertaking, are all evangelical realities, all genuine attempts to bring about the true reign of God on earth. Camilo and Che were helping to bring about this reign by their fight for equal justice for all. They understood that this was their mission, preached, fought and died for it without a trace of opportunism.

They never made any compromise or tried to barter with their consciences. They merely accepted all the consequences which their beliefs entailed, as those beliefs were derived from logical convictions too self-evident to be debated.

Both were highly educated and had a powerful personality. Both were born leaders. Their most outstanding characteristic was their unconditional renunciation of everything, in order to serve the best of causes. Their home was all South America, that vast continent which cries out for justice.

They became revolutionaries and guerrilla fighters because imperialism leads to violence, feeds on violence, is born of violence, and can only be fought with violence. Like all other revolutionaries, Che Guevara and Father Camilo were the offspring of the time and circumstance of their continent.

Che Guevara and Father Camilo are both symbols and prophets of our age. They redeem it with their blood and their example. They died to redeem the times we live in. They set off for the mountains and stayed there, new Christs of the new Christianity. The soldiers hid their bodies in an unknown place, for tyrants fear the bones of heroes. Heroes, even dead, burn only too brightly, while tyrants carry their curse everywhere branded on their foreheads.

Heroes like Che Guevara and Camilo Torres are born when they die; tyrants die when they are born, for they are nothing more than walking corpses. They and their so-called democracies are a negation of every value, while men like Che and Camilo are completely authentic. Their voice, their wounds, their inner fire continue to urge the wretched of the earth to fight, because it is necessary to fight.

When the history of the revolution is written, it will be divided into two parts: the period which preceded the deaths of Che and Camilo, and the period which came after their ultimate sacrifice. From now on, the history of America is split into two halves.

GERMAN GUZMAN CAMPOS (Colombia)

Che Guevara,
many people asked you :
Where is your real home?
And you replied :
My home is where I can fight the revolution.

Your home is where people suffer,
and you can join in their struggle.
Oh, Che, your home is America,
and the footprints you leave on your way to battle
trace the frontiers of your country.
For guerrillas on the march, all day all night,
outline the map of their true nationality.

There, wherever humanity cries out
and its anger catches fire,
and it strikes out at the enemy,
there is your home.
It's true, Che, that you were born
in one specific point in space;
but your heart made you a citizen
of all the horizons of life.

And Cuba, what about Cuba?
Cuba is the home of my heart.
Yet for the sake of the revolution
I gave up my duties, my home and my house.

I even gave up my nationality,
to set off again, taking only the uniform
I had worn in bygone days.
But Cuba will always be mingled
with all of me, each drop of blood;
so how can I really part from Cuba?
Oh, Fidel, Cuba is home!

And Vietnam, what about Vietnam?
Vietnam is a land I never went to,
and yet I have been there. With its selflessness and its sacrifice,
my heart is there in the line of fire.
And what the world needs is at least two or three
or more Vietnams. You once said this,
and *meant* it . . .
As you blew on the coals of the revolution,
until they grew red and glowed.

And now, Che Guevara,
you have fallen on that path of fire and blood;
while you were forging real homes for people,
you were struck down on the road you had chosen.
And as you fell your long arms stretched out to the whole of America.
There are millions left to love you,
and hearts everywhere to remember you,
all those who love the people and the truth you loved.
Some names fill us with pride in humanity.
Some fighters can go on giving strength when they have fallen;
which is why you, Oh, Che, are with us right now in the battle-line.

CU HUY CAN (North Vietnam)

The death of Che Guevara places a responsibility on all revolutionaries of the world to redouble their decision to fight on to the final defeat of imperialism. This is not the time to make long speeches dedicated to Che's memory, but a time for practical, courageous action . . .

Che explained clearly that there is no need to talk more, that the contradictions in the world are clear, and that the time has come for each to take his place in the fight . . .

That is why — in essence — Che Guevara is not dead. I do not wish to speak of Che as if he were dead. It would not make sense. His ideas are with us.

I never met Che Guevara in person, but I know him. And I know him even better now. The important thing is to realise that his ideas are with us, and that is why we are prepared to go on fighting.

STOKELY CARMICHAEL (USA)

★

Che's life has had the virtue of impressing even his worst ideological enemies and making them admire him. It is an almost unique example of how a man has been able to gain the recognition and respect of his enemies, of the very troops whom he has faced arms in hand; of his ideological enemies, who have been, surprisingly, almost unanimous in expressing feelings of admiration for Che.

Who could deny the significance to the revolutionary movement of the blow of Che's death, the significance of not being able to count upon his experience, his inspiration, upon that strength of his prestige that all reactionaries feared? It is a fierce blow, a very hard one; however, we are sure that he, more than anyone, was convinced that it is not the physical life of men, but their conduct which counts. That alone can explain his own absolute scorn for danger. That alone accounts for his personality and his actions. . . .

Che was unsurpassed both as a leader and as a soldier; militarily speaking, he was an extraordinarily able, courageous and warlike guerrilla. His one weak spot was that he was too brave and too indifferent to danger.

His enemies now claim to see a moral in the fact that he should have died. But Che was an artist in guerrilla warfare; he proved it a thousand times over. And yet there are now some to suggest that his glorious and heroic death proves that his concepts and his theories on guerrilla warfare were neither valid nor correct.

The artist can die, especially when his art is the dangerous art of revolutionary warfare, but what cannot possibly die is the art to which he dedicated his life and his intelligence.

Is it surprising that such an artist as Che should die in battle? What is far more astonishing is that he should have survived so many battles during our revolutionary war in which he risked his life countless times. . . .

Che did not die defending any interest or cause other than that of the exploited and downtrodden of this continent. Che died defending that cause alone, and even his worst enemies have not dared to suggest otherwise.

Seen in historical terms, those who act as Che did, who do all they can and who sacrifice everything to the cause of the needy, cannot fail to grow in significance every day and to sink deeper and deeper into the hearts of the people.

FIDEL CASTRO (Cuba)

There will be poems in his memory. But the grinding predicament of *les damnés de la terre* is not lyrical. Nor even the struggle against it, which was Guevara's struggle. Guerrilla warfare, as he explained, is slow, patient, prosaic. It is technical.

Revolutions too are technical. They run the same risks as speculative machines. History defines their rules and their possibilities. It is common knowledge — Castro knew it, Che knew it — that in the past the moment of victory has often masked the moment of defeat. Batista (the king, the tsar, the Kuomintang) are negligible enemies compared to bonapartism and bureaucracy, the hookworms which linger for years in the entrails of the triumphant revolution.

In Cuba the Fidelistas — the authentic originals whose idealism was imperishable and whose ideology was relatively eclectic — have remained indispensable to the integrity of the revolution. They have stood between the people and the opportunists and placemen, the new class : who also suffered in their time.

Yet while Castro stayed, Che departed. Of course, he was not a Cuban. And he could not rest while the United States loomed over Latin America like an umbrella, dripping with greed. Asian communism had made the century its own; the millions had surfaced. So Che abandoned the revolution in favour of the revolution.

Garibaldi, in his greatness, was comic and flamboyant. His insurgents wore red shirts and sang while they marched. Che moved patiently and reflectively, like an underground river. Byronic, certainly. But he also embodied the technique of the age. In Che temperament and social strategy converged. In order to win, he

54

vanished, fell silent, except to the people he went among, who are known to us only as statistics and as possible inhabitants of a landscape which can be seen from an aeroplane.

Not by any stretch of paradox can his failure be called a success. The dialectic is not a conjuror. One cannot even say: his memory and example will live on, like Garibaldi's. That is not enough, for Garibaldi's cause was never won.

DAVID CAUTE (England)

BALLAD

Where the dry river runs
The soldiers took their time;
He could not breathe or climb
When they ringed him in their guns

Two soldiers scrubbed
The school where he was shot
For farmers who could not
Read might read in blood:

And those who live by the word will die by the sword
And their bodies will be burned either alive or dead
Like a new book that must not be read
By a people who should never have been taught to read
Because the word of law and order is the only book they need

Mother mother see your son
What do his wounds say
Only he should not have gone
Not have gone to play

Out beyond the streets we know
Out beyond the town
Till the bullets that he sowed
Grew up in a thousand guns to cut him down

He could have lived by the word and shunned the sword
And his body would have been cherished alive or dead
He could have written books that would have been read and read
By later children who'd have learned to read
Because time to grow is all a child and all a world need

But where could he find rest?
Writing in the east
Hunted by the police
Tortured till he confessed

Where those who live by the word are tried by the sword
And their bodies are buried either alive or dead
Like a new book that must not be read
By a people who oughtn't to be free to read
Because the word of law and order is the only book they need

Or here in the easy west,
Where he could live at least
Writing books in peace
Well fed and well dressed

Where those who live by the word are afraid of the word
And their bodies are constricted alive or dead
By a dread they won't be read or won't be fit to be read

Out beyond the streets we know
Out beyond the town
Till the bullets that he sowed
Grew up in a thousand guns to cut him down

And yet the dead man still
Is with his wounds alive
Will with his wounds survive
The dictator's will
And the rich man's mind
Who when he will not give
To let the poor man live
Turns and sees behind
A man with a broken knife
A man not pure or good
A slaughtered man, whose blood
Pays for the rich man's life
Pays for the rich man's life

ALASDAIR CLAYRE (England)

Fleet through the forest trees
Ran Che Guevara
Moccasined were his feet
Round his cigar a
Beard curled in devil's horns
Brushed by the clutching thorns
Soundless he rushed, a breeze
Shaking the mighty seat
Of McNamara

Camped in the Mountain's heart
With his guerrillas
Bold Che Guevara sat
In his stone pillars
Taunting the Government
Mocking the Conscripts sent
To tear his world apart
Somewhere a rifle spat
Che faced his killers

Men from the C.I.A.
Knives in their garter
Fell on the hero band
Dreaming of Sparta
Loosed off a fusillade
Swift through the Everglade
In brown Bolivian clay
Cuba's bright star, outmanned,
Died like a martyr

DON COLLIS (England)

Companion of my soul, I want to be the
weeping gardener of the soil that covers
you and that, so young, you feed.
Miguel Hernández

So that your corpse may not be the end of you
or your bones a pile of stubble, useful to the tree

65

that must grow where you rot, sleeping soundly,
your universal heart pumping blood in and out
so as not to cry like defenceless orphans in corners
so as not just to sit here, in our minds avenging your loss
on this night, this irremediable night that almost chokes us,
so that you should not have missed the point nor made a bet
in which you lost the lucky number of the victory,
we shall now print your name upon this date.

I want to say that you exist in a way
which is the opposite of existence as we know it,
neither austere nor aggressive, merely silent.
There is no life there, no shouting and fighting,
no manifestos to organize;
they don't have beards there, nor legendary heroes.
It is a life we recreate for you so that we need not face
the sight of you, broken and stiff and dead.
This is the only tolerable theory,
everything else hurts too much;
as if they had cut off a limb from each of us.
Our feet go nowhere, only towards the memory
you left behind, the popular cemetery where you are buried
a second time, with your wide-open eyes.
The head is useless, we can't bear it on our shoulders,
it rolled with you when your luck ran out.

They defeated you once guerrilla,
but only once, not more
just enough time to arm our suffering
with tears and everything you need to kill.
Your death starts another cycle of anger,
we are going to recover your heritage bullet by bullet,
each footprint marked by your boot on the American woodland,
your asthma with open mouth, your love that sustains us,
your violence and your indispensable hatred,
your throat full of tender words.

I Salute you man of God!
though you will not listen to the arrogance
of a man who loves every bit of you.
We will never see you again

dreaming of continents.
Sustain our vengeance from that solitude,
from that mineral deep where the mystery is denser.
One fruitful, luminous day . . .
YOUR GREAT ADVENTURE WILL SWEEP THE WORLD.
There immortality resides,
companion of my soul, companion,
hasta la victoria siempre.

ANTONIO CONTE (Cuba)

Now words will be written, useless words, eloquent words, dictated by tears or by anger; now beautiful images will be composed about phoenixes rising from the ashes; now there will be poems and discussions which will be dedicated to the image of Che. I'm writing words too, but I don't want my words to be like those. I don't want to be someone writing words about him. I ask for the impossible, that which I least deserve, that which I dared do once when he was alive : I ask that it be his voice recorded here, that it be his hand that writes these lines. I know this is absurd, impossible; and that is exactly why I feel he is writing these lines with me, because no one knew better than he to what extent the absurd, the impossible, would one day become a reality for mankind, that future for which he gave his young, his marvellous life. Use my hand once more, then, my brother. It has done them no good to cut off your hands, it has done them no good to kill you and hide you away with such infamous cunning. Take my pen, and write. What I say and do I will say and do with you at my side. Only thus does it make sense to go on living.

JULIO CORTAZAR (Argentina)

I want to point out, first of all, that Guevara's death does not mean the end of the struggle against imperialism so much as its beginning; for his death has inexorably furnished a flag to fight under.

Because Che is not one of those who can die — as an example and a guide, he is immortal — because he will live on in the heart of each revolutionary.

One Che has died : others are about to be born or on the point of acting : others are already in action or will enter the stage tomorrow, here and in other parts of the continent. . . .

A civilian lawyer expressed the fear that the defence would ask for clemency, thus depriving the victors of their right to judge the vanquished. But who is asking for clemency? Who presumes to talk in terms of victors? Who admits to being vanquished? Che vanquished because he died? For years, Che had been exposing his life and escaping death by a miracle; years ago, he decided to fight in the front line wherever he might be needed, here and elsewhere; years ago, Che accepted the prospect of dying at any moment. He used to say that his sacrifice would mean nothing, that it would be no more than one incident in the course of world revolution, and that it was up to every one of us to turn his blood into seed. Some men are more dangerous dead than alive, even when those who fear them cut the hands from their corpse, burn the body and hide the ashes. Che comes to life for us now, and the revolution goes on.

No, I will not ask for the clemency of the vanquished. I will not address myself to you as to the victors. On the contrary, I will say to you that, even though I feel I am completely innocent of all the charges you have brought against me, I am guilty of believing in the final and imminent victory of Che. I am guilty of wanting to fulfil the engagement which I contracted towards him, irrevocably; as everyone who had the privilege of seeing Che live, think and act, felt engaged within his limitations to remain loyal to Che and to follow his example, until the end.

I will do all I can to deserve some day the unwarranted honour which you do me when you condemn me for doing what I did not do but which I want, more than ever, to do. And so, calmly and with all my heart, I thank you in advance for the heavy sentence that I expect from you.

I have finished.

REGIS DEBRAY (France), *at his trial at Camiri in November, 1967.*

Che was the first man to show us that we could be disgusted with peaceful co-existence without falling into the trap of right-wing opportunism, that we could reject the petty-bourgeois Marxism of local elections and 'deals' and still remain communists. Above all, he was the first to proclaim loudly and clearly that socialism is worth nothing when it is limited to an economic doctrine which only makes a more rational use of 'the worn-out tools of capitalism,' but what we have to fight for is a socalism which will create a new humanity. We also have Che to thank for the fact that the Cuban Revolution, which gave us new faith and courage in 1959, has continued to remain so dear to our hearts.

Che stands for romanticism without illusions; he stands for the greatest love, that which cannot limit itself to one woman, one man, one family. His is the mad and reasonable love which leads a man to fight on foreign soil, which leads a Jew to fight for the Arabs, a French-man to fight for the Algerians, a white man to fight for the negroes, and a bourgeois to fight for the proletariat. . . .

I can still hear the first thing he ever said to me, nearly seven years ago when I met him in Cuba at the Bay of Pigs during the invasion. 'What are you doing here, Francesa?' I gave a vague explanation . . . 'Paris boring, nothing happening politically. . . .' In that friendly and ironic way of his, he answered, 'But if you can't do anything in France, why not go and fight for the Algerians, who haven't got their independence yet?' Three years later in Algiers, after Algerian inde-pendence, he reminded me of this. 'What are you doing here now? They're free. They don't need you any more.' He also said to me once, 'You like success, what has been won already. You only write about what's victorious. You should fight for a cause which is only just starting, which seems likely to fail. . . .'

It was difficult not to feel shy with him even when you knew him well; you did not feel like using the familiar 'tu' with him, even though everyone addresses the Cuban leaders like that. There was something extraordinarily calm and gentle about Che; his voice was very low, slightly hoarse. I think he was a bit shy himself. What was odd was the contrast between his athletic, muscular frame, and his excessively delicate, aristocratic features, his pale, almost sickly complexion. He was as handsome and attractive as people have made him out to be, but it was not so much his good looks as his expression, so intelligent, kind and humorous, which gave him such charm. He always wore an olive green uniform, thick laced-up boots and a black beret pulled right down over his eyes, never wearing anything else throughout his stay in Paris in 1964. Yet he always looked very neat and never seemed to be in 'fancy dress.' I remember the contrast between his way of dressing and Ben Bella's when we were in Algiers, at the height of China's prestige. Ben Bella wore a uniform which was a curious cross between Nehru's and Mao's, and which Che glanced at with amusement and surprise.

When Che looked at you in that way, you saw yourself for what you were, reduced to your true dimensions. It was impossible to play-act in front of him, to show off what a good little revolutionary you were. You would start talking straight, and Che would listen to you seriously, wrinkling his forehead and for ever chewing a cigar. And as he watched your face carefully, with just a touch of irony in his big almond-shaped eyes, you would feel the need to select your words with care and to express yourself soberly.

I am not trying to give a bird's eye view of history by describing my personal impression of one man; but after all, history is made by men and it is only human beings who retain impressions which they can transmit. And Che, who is now becoming a folk legend, was first and foremost a man, a man of the next century, a man of the future, an authentic communist who kept us from losing all hope. Che has really lived; while Che continues to live in our minds and to help us all become better, outdo ourselves, all is still possible.

ANIA FRANCOS (France)

I am writing to you, comrade, from a faraway continent, where men aren't happy. We suffer from working and not knowing for whom or why; from producing things that are only measured in terms of money or comfort; from being occupied eight to nine hours a day in exchange for a salary that, no matter how high it is, will never make up for the monotony of our work. We suffer from not being able to contribute, seventeen hours a day, the best of ourselves in exchange only for the happiness of testing the limit of our strength in the common battle against all that degrades mankind, and the happiness of seeing — both in the look of our comrades and in the mark of our imprint on the struggle to be equal, each one for all — that world which is about to be made.

I am writing to you, comrade, from a faraway continent, to tell you that we envy you. You have confirmed what we knew without recognising it; that the only fatherland of the revolutionary is the revolution; that love of liberty must turn into implacable hatred against all those who confuse freedom with their own self interest; that socialism is the negation of money, of commercial relations and of the straight division of labour; that each man can be saved and that he makes history from the moment he triumphs, even for one instant and losing his life in the process, over the forces of inhumanity which still dominate the world.

I am writing to you, comrade, from a faraway continent, to tell you that from the moment a man like you is bold enough to appear, he discovers and reveals to others that he is not alone but one of hundreds, perhaps thousands, with new and invincible ideas. I, who am not a Christian, am telling you that your assassins suffer from the same illusions as the Romans, who one thousand nine hundred and thirty years ago, executed, next to two bandits, a Jewish agitator who had not got with him more than a dozen men; his ideas have triumphed all the same over the imperial state which then dominated the world. That will happen to you too, comrade, because it must be so. But it saddens me that you should not see that day; I am saddened not for you, who took the idea of death lightly and considered yourself absolutely replaceable, but for all of us on whom falls the terrible and difficult privilege of outliving you.

ANDRE GORZ (France)

The death of Che Guevara brought a sense of grief and disappointment to people who had no Marxist sympathies. He represented the idea of gallantry, chivalry and adventure in a world more and more given up to business arrangements between the great world powers; he expressed for us the hope that victory did not always go to the big battalions. One found among the most conservative a genuine sorrow that numbers and weapons had won again, and that the adventure of the twelve in Cuba had not been repeated. Was this the end of the forlorn hope, the fight against odds? But the circumstances of Che's death begin to give us comfort. That he was shot after capture demonstrates the fear that the Bolivian authorities felt even of an imprisoned Che. They were afraid to bring him to trial : afraid of the echoes his voice would have aroused from the courtroom : afraid to prove that the man they hated was loved by the world outside. This fear will help to perpetuate his legend, and a legend is impervious to bullets.

GRAHAM GREENE (England)

Not because you've fallen
does your light shine less brightly.
Your guerrilla's silhouette
sits astride a horse of fire
between the wind and clouds of the Sierra.
You are not silent although they've hushed you up.
And although they burn you,
although they hide you underground,
although they conceal you
in cemeteries, forests, mountains,
they won't stop us from finding you,
Che Comandante,
friend.

Nicolás Guillén

Little soldier of Bolivia,
Little Bolivian soldier,
you go armed with your rifle,
which is an American rifle,
which is an American rifle,
little soldier of Bolivia,
which is an American rifle.

It was given to you by Señor Barrientos,
little Bolivian soldier,
a present from Mister Johnson
to kill your brother,
to kill your brother,
little soldier of Bolivia,
to kill your brother.

You don't know who is the dead man?
little Bolivian soldier?
The dead man is Che Guevara,
and he was Argentine and Cuban,
and he was Argentine and Cuban,
little soldier of Bolivia,
and he was Argentine and Cuban.

He was your best friend,
little Bolivian soldier,

he was the friend of the poor
from the oriente to the altiplano
from the oriente to the altiplano
little soldier of Bolivia
from the oriente to the altiplano

The whole of my guitar
little Bolivian soldier,
is in mourning, but not crying,
though to cry is human,
though to cry is human,
little soldier of Bolivia,
though to cry is human.

This is no time to cry
little Bolivian soldier,
we need no tears nor hankies
but a machete in the hand,
but a machete in the hand,
little soldier of Bolivia,
but a machete in the hand.

With the coppers that they pay you,
little Bolivian soldier,
they sell you and they buy you
that's what the tyrants think,
that's what the tyrants think,
little soldier of Bolivia,
that's what the tyrants think.

Wake up the time has come,
little Bolivian soldier,
and all the world sits up,
because the sun has risen early,
because the sun has risen early,
little soldier of Bolivia,
because the sun has risen early.

Take the right road,
little Bolivian soldier,
it isn't always the easy road,

it isn't always easy or smooth,
it isn't always easy or smooth,
little soldier of Bolivia,
it isn't always easy or smooth.

But you are bound to learn
little Bolivian soldier,
that a brother must not be killed
that you musn't kill a brother,
that you musn't kill a brother,
little soldier of Bolivia,
that you mustn't kill a brother.

NICOLAS GUILLEN (Cuba)

The cause of Fidel and Che has become the cause of all future communism, the kind of communism which has never been put into practise anywhere and which would perhaps do well not to call itself communism while it forges a new method of combat more in keeping with the new situation in which we find ourselves. The history of the Cuban Revolution clearly shows what we can already hope for in the future: to stop dwelling obsessively on the events and difficulties of the past, and to stimulate the trust, imagination and initiative of everyone in every walk of life.

The ever growing interest that European intellectuals feel in the Third World is not, as some might believe, merely ' escapism ' nor a romantic delusion which has no connection with the problems confronting them. It is the bourgeoisie (along with a few so-called left-wingers who don't realise that they are repeating all the bourgeois slogans) which would like to pass off Régis Debray as a new Lord Byron whose wish to do good is both naïve and old-fashioned. It is also the bourgeoisie which would like to compare El Che to Jesus Christ in order to vitiate the political significance of his ideas and his life.

In fact, authentic revolutionary European intellectuals are internationalists like all other authentic revolutionaries everywhere else. These revolutionary intellectuals of Europe are aware of the fact that their battles cannot be waged on the same level as in Latin America, and this is the major issue which they have to resolve. For obviously ideas cannot have the same impact on industrialised nations as on underdeveloped ones. Words as well as attitudes have to be adapted to different circumstances. But European intellectuals do follow the progress of the revolutionary struggles in the Third World with tremendous attention. For that is the only way in which they can define their own attitudes both towards society and for themselves.

It is largely thanks to the Third World that European intellectuals have been able to discover today who they are, what they want and why they want it. The revolutionary individual within a capitalistic society is like a Third World all of his own : his particular tactics must be like those of a guerrilla fighter, always changing terrain and breaking out of the official cultural channels which try to encircle him. A cultural revolution is taking place in China; tomorrow, we could have a cultural guerrilla war all over Europe. I think this would be a good thing because it might then lead to the emergence of a new culture which would eventually give birth to the New Man Che Guevara spoke about : the individual in a state of permanent revolt.

ALAIN JOUFFROY (France)

Week of Che Guevara, hunted, hurt,
held prisoner one lost day, then gangstered down
for gold, for justice — violence cracking on violence,
like rock on rock, the corpse of the last armed prophet
laid out on a sink in a shed, displayed by flashlight —
as the leaves light up, still green, this afternoon,
and burn to balding reds; as the oak, lop-branched
to go on living, swells with goitres like a fruit-tree,
as the walls of the high white stone buildings over-
awe the poor, too good for this new world,
this New York, where our clasped, illicit hands
pulse, stop the bloodstream, as if it hit rock . . .
Rest them for the outlaw . . . kings once hid in oaks,
with prices on their heads, and watched for game.

(This is what it is, and no more a tribute to Che than Shakespeare's Hotspur is a tribute.)

ROBERT LOWELL (USA)

HAIKU FOR CHE

December. Late birds shake their wings.
On the snowy windscreen of a car, I write
CHE LIVES!

CHRISTOPHER LOGUE (England)

The revolutionary
Believed in revolution —
Even in art. What was real
Was too good for ' realism '. Burn
L'art pompier! Such a smell
As those waxworks flared, and their glass
Eyes dropped from the sockets and rolled
On the floor, gleefully winking.
Only what was alive would do.

Yet he died, and the photograph
His enemies took of him showed
A face that looked like wax. He lay
There on the rough boards — a dummy
Which even resemblance had left.

The thing is, one shouldn't accept
What one's enemies make of one.
They killed you, Che. But your mind lives,
And it speaks as plainly. No wax
For you, no frozen heroic
Poses. Merely a name which now,
When we speak it, honours mankind.

EDWARD LUCIE-SMITH (England)

When this great dishonour looming over Latin America is paid for,
When this great shame is washed away with the good soap made from
       the blood of heroes,
When freedom no longer means wads of dollars and deceit,
Then comrades you'll see how a phoenix rises from its ashes,
And it doesn't matter if the same sun which shines now on the tomb
       of the fallen guerrilla
Shines on the sterile sword of the sad sad generals.

Man, why this anger, woman, why these tears?
Don't you know that a hero must die, and that the beautiful wind must
       blow him away?
The hero had a message too urgent to wait,
and a watchfulness too full of protest,
In other words an irritating menace and a nuisance.
Which is why when the hero falls the wicked rejoice full face,
while the wary common people ache in profile.
Oh, Che, you won't see me weeping over your defeated flesh,
Because yet again I look at the scales where the balance of your last
       battle is weighed;
And looking at these scales I can say to your enemies and ours:
' You have turned a fallible guerrilla into an infallible force,
And that force which cannot falter is coming to life in Santa Cruz,
And is already setting the rhythm of future battles.'

                    LEOPOLDO MARECHAL (Argentina)

CHE'S TALE

Che once told the story
Of how during a fight
A man called for silence
' Without knowing why,'
       (was Che's comment)

It's now become a legend
That in this continent
People shouldn't remain silent

Which is why El Che,
Gun smoking in his hand
His finger on the trigger,
To the Andes went . . .
                    (and now is silent)
                    MANUEL DIAZ MARTINEZ (Cuba)

AN IMPERSONAL NOTE TO CHE GUEVARA

I don't know what you were like.
I've looked at the photos,
Read what Fidel had to say,
Gone through your books, speeches.

I've got a feeling that if I'd met you,
I might have found you arrogant, or mad.
So what I say about you is not personal,
Nor do I want to be you, now or later.

I just want to say that my mind is richer for your thoughts,
My humanity prouder for your actions,
My life less acceptable for your death,
My death more acceptable for your life.
                    JOHN McGRATH (England)

Anyone who has experiencd the Cuban Revolution at first hand, who
has talked with workers and peasants and their revolutionary leaders,
must have been nauseated by the vicious column in the *Daily Mail*
written by Bernard Levin at the time of ' Che ' Guevara's death. One
would not normally waste time on the hysterical and ignorant rubbish
which pours from Levin's pen when he contemplates the ' undemo-
cratic ' regime of Castro, and the ' murderous ' and ' terroristic ' activities of Guevara. However, Levin also vented a certain amount of

spleen on what he described as ' the fools in the West . . .' who support the Cuban Revolution and admired Guevara. Behind his choleric emotions, cheapness of language, and indifference to rational analysis, Levin speaks no doubt for the ' wise '. For those, that is to say, who cannot stomach violent revolution in the first place and who believe in any case that a revolutionary government will turn out to be as vile, if not more so, than the tyranny it has overthrown.

There are chilling precedents which superficially justify this conviction — but the case of Cuba, and the meaning of Guevara, deserve more careful examination. If there is to be revolutionary conflict in Latin America and elsewhere in the second half of this century — and this is virtually certain — we cannot afford the luxury of liberal denunciation, but must analyse the actual historical processes leading to death, violence and terror. We cannot afford a morality unilluminated by a profound understanding of the conditions in which men are prepared to fight and die rather than subsist in a ' peace ' which keeps them economically and spiritually on their knees. The subtleties and dilemmas of intellectuals who operate from a comfortable distance, and *in* the comfort of materially advanced societies, become nothing more than a kind of historical voyeurism. The ' fools in the West ' at least recognise this, and conclude that a political philosophy and morality which will not come to terms with the necessary overthrow of capitalist penetration and domination in the Third World, is sterile. But the foolish and the wise alike may find themselves, in the coming upheavals, as irrelevant as the ladies who took their picnic baskets to the Crimean heights to watch a battle or two in civilised security.

There has been without doubt a certain amount of myth-making about Guevara in the West and elsewhere. This is not to say that Che was anything less than his legend, but rather that his combination of revolutionary idealism and concrete action have had a considerable impact on the scepticism which has perniciously undermined engaged opinion throughout the world. In so far as he was an exponent of violence, it was a counter-violence to that of entrenched reactionary authority whose crimes, tortures and suppressions of popular resistance in Latin America are beyond question. Of course, the violence of the revolution is ' terrorism ' by Western terms of reference. For every statistic of fascist savagery, there seems to be an equally horrifying statistic of revolutionary terror to cancel it out — as if human suffering were explicable in some sort of ideological profit and loss account. Peasants in the Sierra Maestra and workers in the Cuban towns required no indoctrination to understand that nothing short of violent opposition would put an end to the Batista regime. What is more, they came to realise in the course of their struggle — a discovery shared by Castro and Guevara — that simply to eliminate the Batista regime would not be enough. Their needs determined their social objectives, and their needs required the termination of the colonial status of Cuba vis-à-vis the USA.

Once this had been achieved, Guevara felt compelled to move on — to carry the struggle, and his analysis of his Cuban experience, onto the main continent. It is natural for those who feel helpless in Europe to identify with the potent image of an intellectual, a humanist and a fighter whose actions are consistent with his words. We do not make history, we are insulated from it — trapped in our lives, our culture, and the sickening momentum of technological transformation which throws up nothing human and offers only a kind of pseudo-liberation for privileged individuals. Most people work and live and die much as they always have, except in greater material comfort. Vision has sunk to the horizons of politicians and technocrats, of managers and education-factories. The meagre liberation of the few is into an almost narcissistic recognition of their paralysis, failure, apathy — and even understanding and insight seem to lead finally to an agonised shrug or a hysterical shout.

But Guevara's life is a reminder of what is possible, of what is being done. We are closing up for what may be the last and most implacable confrontation of all — that between the humiliated poor and the arrogant rich, on an international scale. Nothing short of revolution will overcome underdevelopment, yet what will overcome the armed hostility of the USA and the West in general, to revolution? And will the Soviet Union continue to hover uncertainly between the turbulence in Asia and Latin America, and the bigoted ferocity in Washington? Are we to see these historical contradictions through the eyes of Che Guevara, or simply with the compassionate yet abdicating resignation of people accustomed to understanding much and doing little?

The significance of Che is not a solution but a question.

DAVID MERCER (England)

LETTERS TO CHE: CANTO BILINGUE

Te escribo cartas, Che,
En la sazon de lluvias
Envenenadas

They came without faces
Found you with eyeless rays
The tin grasshoppers
With five-cornered magic
Wanting to feed you
To the man-eating computer

Te escribo cartas, Guerrero,
Vestido de hojas y lunas

But you won and became
The rarest jungle tree
A lost leopard
Out of metal's way

Te escribo cartas
Hermano invisible
Gato de la noche lejana

Cat of far nights
Whisper of a Bolivian kettle
Cry
Of an Inca hill

Te escribo cartas, Niño
De la musica callada.

THOMAS MERTON (USA)

HOW TO KILL CUBA

You must burn the people first.
Then the grass and trees, then the stones.
You must cut the island out of all the maps,
The history books, out of the old newspapers,
Even the newspapers which hated Cuba,

And burn all these, and burn
The paintings, poems and photographs and films
And when you have burnt all these
You must bury the ashes
You must guard the grave
And even then
Cuba will only be dead like Che Guevara —
Technically dead, that's all,
Technically dead.

ADRIAN MITCHELL (England)

The way he lived and died is a saga, of the twentieth century. It tells me : Whatever things we fight for ultimately become, they *are* worth dying for. Those who give their life for these things will remain forever a testimony of man's need to overcome his own nature, his own destiny. Without men like Che there would be no more hope left. I believe he knew he would die, but I also feel that death for him was more acceptable than the inevitable compromises a victorious revolution always leads to. A revolution is clean, while it fights against odds. Che wanted to remain clean and has remained so. If there were thousands of Ches, those who make life on earth a misery would probably get scared and leave us in peace. There must be thousands of Ches if we want to survive with dignity.

JIRI MUCHA (Czechoslovakia)

What can I say about Che that has not already been said?

That I remember the night when I got to know him by the light of the fires.

That at one time we were enemies, but in spite of that, I admired him.

That afterwards I asked to work especially with him. And one day I put my hand on his shoulder as a sign of affection and he said to me : Is that trust? And my hand fell.

The days passed and one day he said to me : Do you know? You are not such a bastard as they told me you were. And we laughed and became friends.

What can I say about Che that has not already been said?

That one day I asked him: Haven't you ever known fear? and he answered: A terrible fear.

That in the most sectarian days, an extremist attacked the 26th of July movement, and after thinking about it I said to Che: It is true that we knew nothing about Marxism and we did not belong to the party; but perhaps thanks to that, we were able to pull down Batista.

And we talked things over.

That when I was at my most anti-sectarian and unjustly attacked some old communist, Che told me off.

That once, when someone criticised the shortage of food, he said that it was not true, that in his home they ate reasonably well.

Perhaps you receive an additional quota, I said to him, half-seriously and half-jokingly.

Later he called us to tell us: ' It was true; until yesterday we were getting an additional quota.'

What can I say about Che that has not already been said?

That I remember the early mornings in the Ministry of Industry when we used to joke while waiting for the time to leave for our voluntary work. He used to come at night to Juceplán and after the exhausting meetings he used to play a game of chess with the guards, while we sat round them singing softly, and out of tune, old tangos of his childhood.

That at the beginning he was very strict in the matter of women but ended up by saying that he didn't look after the fly of anybody else's trousers.

That I remember the night when my mother died, when we were not yet real friends, and those who were friends did not come to see me. I remember, I repeat, he arrived at dawn for the funeral and he put his hand on my shoulder, as I had done to him that other time. And he stayed talking to me for hours until it was daytime.

That afterwards, when I no longer worked with him, and went on wishing to see him, each time I went to his office we would talk interminably. Manresa would ask for coffee. Che would throw himself on the floor, on the carpet, smoking. When the air-conditioning broke down, we would open the windows and take our shirts off. We settled the world then. Well, look here, little polack, he would say.

But we were old night-birds and I would not leave until dawn was breaking, and we would go down together in the elevator, he complaining that I made him waste a lot of time.

87

What can I say about Che that has not already been said?

That I have not yet been able to pluck up the courage to go and see Aleida and have a look at the kids.

That when I saw the photographs of Bolivia, he lying on the dais, with his naked body, I remembered the nights when he lay on the carpet in his office, in the Ministry of Industry, with a look that went beyond all things, with a brightness in his eyes like a reflection of the stars, the stars of the South.

What can I say?

ENRIQUE OLTUSKI (Cuba)

GUEVARA IS DEAD . . . LONG LIVE GUEVARA!

'There is no definition of socialism which makes sense for us,' said Che Guevara, 'but the abolition of exploitation of one man by another.' Or of one country by another. The West is Billy Bunter in a world of Oliver Twists and Guevara saw no boundaries; for exploiters are running free in Athens and Djakarta, Saigon and the Congo. So he taught tin miners to throw dynamite, mountain Indians to use their traps for war. The Doctor took up a carbine (yet lagged behind the guerrilla bands of the Cuban Revolution to care for the wounded on both sides). Men like Guevara are too big and angry for our world of typewriters and soft hands; too big for the court-room of Camiri, too honest for those fat men in the Kremlin who ordered their parties to betray the guerrillas and whose revolution goes on in drapes and velours, and too serious to live into middle age.

OZ MAGAZINE (England)

The death of Jack Kennedy was painful to intellectuals less because they admired him than because they believed that he admired them. Guevara's death is not painful in this sense; no intelligent person living in an advanced country except in a state of total dissent (and how many can achieve or sustain that condition?) can fail to realise, without grievous self-deception, that he is, by the very fact of his comfortable existence, someone whom Guevara would not have admired, whom Guevara *accuses*. Guevara's death may create a myth; it also removes a critic. . . .

No question about it. I am not fighting for the starving or the oppressed except, fitfully, with words, guiltily, patronisingly, with gifts. I am as inclined as most to fall into the ritual posture of stagey solidarity when faced with Guevara's example. He makes Verkhovenskys of us all. Make no mistake : I do not especially blame myself. Objectively, it is impossible to do right in the present world situation so long as one accepts (by one's life, not one's words) the divisions of rich and poor. We literally owe the world to the destitute and the oppressed, who still compose the vast majority, and Guevara, who was both an educated man (education being itself almost a reproach and yet the only hope) and a completely dispossessed person, demonstrated the possibility of a bridge between the two irreconcilables of rich and poor. The assumption that the problem is too big for individual action reveals the degree of alienation from which we now suffer. We, the important, rule ourselves out as serious contributors to the world struggle and leave it to the poor to be real. As Wittgenstein endlessly pointed out, nothing can be true in the world unless it is possible for it also to be false; the saying can be reversed : we are in the situation of scarcely even being able meaningfully to be false, since there is scarcely any sense in which we can be true. Guevara is almost meaningless to us as an example : in the global village, everything is happening at the other end of town and, if we are honest about our reactions, we thank our gods for it.

FREDERIC RAPHAEL (USA)

In Cuba the image of Che Guevara is everywhere, on gigantic posters and postage stamps, in offices and shops, in books and periodicals of every kind. Che, a guerrilla leader and hero in his lifetime, has become by virtue of his tragic death, a martyr and secular saint.

From Cuba this hero-worship spreads throughout Central and South America. Even in Puerto Rico, dominated as it is by American capital and propaganda, the image of Che appears surreptitiously on lamp-posts and hoardings.

For the first time in its history the communist movement has found a *romantic* hero, a hero in the tradition of Count Roland or the Black Prince; a *political* hero as charismatic as Mickiewicz or Garibaldi. But to the people of Latin America he is more than any hero of the past. He is the ideal human being, physically beautiful, morally clean, and politically incorruptible.

The last hero remotely comparable to Che was Lawrence of Arabia, but Lawrence was an ambiguous figure — sexually ambiguous and politically indecisive. Che was a happily married man with five children and his political ideals were precise and precisely formulated. He had *style,* in his life and actions, in his thought and writing. He was gay and affectionate, and his love embraced the poor and oppressed of the whole world.

When the Revolution triumphed in Cuba and he could look forward to a life of comparative ease and power, he renounced it. The Revolution could not end in Cuba; it must be carried to Cuba's neighbouring peoples, to every country where the working classes were enslaved and exploited.

Impossible to doubt Che's idealism; impossible not to admire his courage and self-sacrifice.

But it is legitimate to express doubts about his methods, his revolutionary strategy. Moral doubts and political doubts.

Che Guevara believed in the necessity of violence to achieve his revolutionary aims. I am a pacifist and believe that violence is morally wrong and politically inexpedient.

Castro's and Che's tactics of violence were successful in Cuba, but the more one learns about what happened in Cuba nine years ago, the more evident becomes the element of pure chance that ensured a victory for those tactics. Batista's régime was so corrupt that it was ready to crumble at the first appearance of a popular uprising. The United States was caught napping and was not able to crush the Revolution before Castro had secured the active support of Russia. The Bay of Pigs episode was a clumsy fiasco, and the subsequent ' missile crisis ' only served to reveal the impotence of the two giants armed with their obliterative bombs.

Since that confrontation the Cuban Revolution has sheltered under the missile umbrella. The United States has tried to destroy the Revolution by other means, by diplomatic intrigues and savage economic sanctions. But Cuba so far has survived and with every month that passes her political position becomes stronger. Her economic position is still precarious, but provided she is not deserted by the rest of the communist world, she will survive. The social and cultural achievements of the régime are already very impressive, which is another cause for the resentment of her enemies.

The missile umbrella is very relevant to the whole question of guerrilla tactics. Che had a pathetic faith in these tactics; so had the majority of the delegates who assembled in Havana for the recent Cultural Congress. But what happened to Che in Bolivia is an illustration of the futility of these tactics. Apart from the fact that they can be employed only under the shelter of the missile umbrella (for one 'strategic weapon' would wipe out any isolated guerrilla action), these tactics depend on the myth of a co-operative peasantry. But everything, even in the Cuban Revolution, goes to show that the peasantry is the most indifferent and even hostile class in a revolutionary situation. The peasant with his three acres and a cow, or whatever may be the regional equivalent, is not militant by nature nor upbringing. He is rooted to the earth and makes a most indifferent activist. I was told in Havana that in Bolivia Che had succeeded in enlisting from the Bolivian countryside only ten peasants. Of these, two had defected and one had betrayed him.

Guerrilla warfare, as a revolutionary strategy, is a romantic myth. In the modern world, even in 'underdeveloped' countries, the only realistic strategy is the general strike of industrial workers. The peasants can hold up food supplies, but that takes months to be effective. The industrial workers — transport, electrical, distributive, sanitary — can paralyse a community in twenty-four hours. Such is a non-violent strategy of revolution, and in all but freak circumstances it is the only strategy.

But there is something more to Che than his romantic reliance on violence. He was above all a humanist, and believed that it was possible to create a 'new man'. Society must be 'a huge school', he said, and he saw the new man beginning to emerge in the period of the building of socialism. 'His image is as yet unfinished; in fact it will never be finished, since the process advances parallel to the development of new economic forms.' But the process was not to be one of brain-washing, of mass propaganda — 'the individual receives the impact of the new social power and perceives that he is not completely adequate to it. Under the influence of the pressure implied in indirect education, he tries to adjust to a situation that he feels to be just and whose lack of development has kept him from doing so thus far. He is educating himself.' As far as the masses are concerned, Che recognised that it would be a long and difficult road, and man can only advance along that road if he breaks the chains of alienation.

'This will be translated concretely into the reappropriation of his nature through freed work and the expression of his own human condition in culture and art.'

There seems to be no doubt that Che Guevara was responsible for the exceptional degree of intellectual and artistic freedom that prevails in Cuba — for the deliberate rejection of a socialist realism based on the bourgeois art of the last century, and the inauguration of a new art worthy of the new man. 'It is the 21st century man we must create, although this is still a subjective and not a realised aspiration. It is not a question of how many kilograms of meat are eaten or how many times a year someone may go on holiday to the sea shore or how many pretty imported things can be bought with present wages. It is rather that the individual feels greater fulfilment, that he has greater inner wealth and many more responsibiities. In our country the individual knows that the glorious period in which it has fallen to him to live is one of sacrifice; he is familiar with sacrifice.'*

It is this emphasis on individualism, found in Castro as well as in Che Guevara, that makes the Cuban Revolution so distinctive and so different from the doctrinaire régimes of the USSR and Eastern Europe. There was nothing dogmatic about Che. He believed that, 'We socialists are more free because we are more fulfilled; we are more fulfilled because we are more free.' His great appeal is based on this spirit of freedom and sacrifice. He also dared to use the word 'love'. 'The true revolutionary,' he pointed out, 'is guided by strong feelings of love. Our vanguard revolutionaries must idealise this love for the peoples, for the most hallowed causes, and make it one and indivisible.'

It would be self-deception to present Che as a libertarian socialist, but in everything he said and did he was nearer to the spirit of Kropotkin and Tolstoy than to that of Lenin and Stalin. Even the stage of guerrilla warfare (and he described it as a 'stage') was seen as 'a catalyst which created the subjective condition necessary for victory.' But 'the individual was also the basic factory in the guerrilla, in the framework of the gradualisation of our thinking, in the revolution taking place in our habits and in our minds.' Without that personal heroism, that individual sense of glory, nothing would have been achieved in Cuba.

HERBERT READ

---

* These quotations come from *Man and Socialism in Cuba,* a translation of *El Socialismo y el Hombre en Cuba* (1965) published by the Book Institute in Havana in 1967.

EL COMANDANTE

So they shot at this left leg with which I'd walked
all over the world; not even a tree
to tell them off, and vipers, vipers
that hiss like bullets : catch him ! crush him !
And the asthma too and one other thing,
so that makes three. The asthma, the asthma. . . .

So that makes three or three o'clock,
and it isn't October and it isn't the eighth,
and that is the way the ravine ends,
the Yuro ravine, and that is the way
the ravine of the world bursts open
and closes over. In October they shot me.

Five thousand dollars (or was it fifty?)
for this blood of mine, and was it for this
that we were and are? They gave five thousand
for my eyes and hands, fifty thousand the lot !
with the asthma thrown in, the bad lungs too,
that were going to sing my fortieth birthday.

The fatal whine of death's mosquitoes
sing ' Up with the poor ! *Arriba!* Fire ! '
Flash of machine-guns, welcome the bullets
if others come after. Quick ! let's run
Quick, oh quick, to avenge the dead man.

Mine, what's mine? This rose, this America,
with all its old thorns. All that dawn
they judged me in English. What's mine is mine,
and yours too, brother. What a blow !
straight in the heart where fear begins.

And so they bled me, then they burnt me,
in Vallegrande — and took me there
in a helicopter — there's nothing wrong
with sprinkling blood to refresh the air,
even though after that they burnt my body,
chopped off both hands : Go on, shoot ! Don't stop !

I'll be back, Bolivar, but now I'm off. . . .

GONZALO ROJAS (Chile)

93

The tense voice of Fernández Retamar sounds and resounds in our ears. In the aeroplane that took us from Mexico to Havana in March, 1967, he was singing

> Here remains the clear
> intimate transparence
> of your dear presence
> Comandante Che Guevara.

We did not know where the verses or the music came from although some of us noted that from their grace and love, they were of Cuban origin. In no other country than Cuba could that quartet have been written or sung, for there that presence of intimate transparency lives with such force.

That was in March. We are now in October. And now that clarity and that transparency, which the Cuban poet was praising, is not only in Cuba. It has extended to all America. The obscene military hand that murdered the man in Vallegrande, did not know how much it was making that presence grow, that clarity, that transparence. The Gorillas of America will disappear in obscurity, sunk in their own abjection or in that of their masters. They will disappear like opaque and dirty shadows.

Ernesto Che Guevara — ' veteran and guerrilla ' as his brother Fidel called him — will become each day more clear, more transparent and more engraved in our hearts and in the land of America.

For all and for ever, glorious and sorrowful; and now I would like to sing in memory of him, with my bad voice the song I heard Fernández Retamar sing : but I cannot. No one can sing in mourning no matter how much clarity there is, and I do not know if I could again.

MANUEL ROJAS (Chile)

THE BEE HIVE

I don't believe in ghosts
yet surgeons transplant a living heart
into the chest cavity of a dead man
a fisty pulping orange
. . . a new ticker !

94

But for a bullet hole in the heart
there is no second valentine for a Marxist.
The worms have murdered the tiger. Che is dead.
And in time, we too shall face the bee keeper
for they who move with tender feet
through the saw-mills of the hive
they shall hear a hymn of Carpenter bees
whose furnace song is dum-dum's liturgy.

In secret ground they've buried Che's dust
trembling like monks who hide religious radium
from the lead eyes of the poor.

J. ROSENBLATT (Canada)

Che Guevara interests me as a writer, as a thinker and as a man of action. To know him, you have to read what he wrote as well as find out the details of his life. Not only were his ideas great ideas; they also had, first and foremost, the coherence of ideas which had been put into practice as well as preached by a man who finally sacrificed his life for them.

Che was not dogmatic, nor was he a demagogue, as is so often the case in the realm of ideas. The very way in which he expressed himself was characteristic : he would speak as though he were seeking a truth within himself that he was trying to communicate to others.

Many intellectuals like myself have splendid ideas, but not all intellectuals have either the moral strength or the physical courage to put their ideas into practice. Che Guevara had this strength and that is why he will go down in history as a great man. He was the link between the Cuban Revolution in action and the revolution over the whole Latin American continent. Cuba can justly feel proud of Che's internationalism, which was the living embodiment of the revolutionary doctrine.

Some ideas are greater than men, but some men are as great as their ideas. I don't just say this because I believe it is true, but because Che Guevara has proved that it is true.

FRANCESCO ROSI (Italy)

EPITAPH TO BE PLACED ON A MAP OF AMERICA

Here lies Ernesto Guevara; they buried him in a box of earth and fear and they covered it up with the skyless night of the forest.

This tomb is in the jagged shape of a map of America : it is trodden by the bare feet of those who bear the shackles of poverty round their ankles and who wear the truth like a grimy halo.

He was a hero and an artist, because an artist is a man who transcends his creation, and a hero's work of art is that last gesture of his life in which he gives up his life in order to kill his death.

At that instant, the idea becomes the ideal, and the ideal then transcends the cold logic of intelligence to attain the mysterious realm of aesthetics; it is there that the ideal becomes one with flesh, becomes one with pain and with fear, and takes on the shape of the act that called it into existence. Thus heroism and art are fused into one and the same thing.

In warfare, Guevara was a humanist; for armed struggle only meant one thing to him : that gesture which America is beginning to make, that gesture of picking up a rifle in battle, a rifle that turns the hand which holds it into a clenched fist.

DALMIRO SAENZ (Argentina)

Che Guevara's life is the finest example of Caribbean-American revolutionary heroism I know; the news of his death, the most humbling and numbing I have experienced, is similar in personal loss to a death in one's own family. His legendary life and tragic death are as much mine, and ours, as they are gloriously his; his life's work and its terrible termination are a revolutionary whole. How acceptable Sartre's rhetoric sounds, now, a matter of months after Che's assassination: ' (He) was not only an intellectual but also the most complete human being of our age.'

Che's heroism has many meanings, and each has its unique importance, because each satisfies our particular memory of his exemplary life and death : as Bolivar's historical heir; Fidel's spiritual other self; the New World's avenging visitor; and as the universal symbol of the modern revolution. Above all, there is his definition of solidarity through direct involvement and action, a demand which few are physically and morally able to meet: 'It is not a matter of wishing success to the victim of aggression, but of sharing his fate; one must accompany him to his death or to victory.'

Very nearly all the lessons drawn from Che's revolutionary struggles, beginning with his and Fidel's intensive guerrilla training in Mexico and continuing in combat in Cuba, and later, alone, in Bolivia, have been instructions in armed acts of solidarity not only to the serving men and women in the hills and in the towns but also to the intellectuals. The peasants and intellectuals, often recalcitrant and inherently conservative, have been crucial elements in the effective unification of all modern revolutionary movements, as Che has always emphasized. His daunting challenge to the intellectuals to become men of decisive armed action has been uncompromising. His lesson, here, is that ideas must lead to action or they will slide back into dreams, and that, equally urgently, action without the salt of ideology ends as empty action. The natural revolutionary intellectual is always hard to come by, and Che knew it.

He also knew that guerrilla confrontations with a monstrous enemy must be spread over the broadest possible area, with highly sensitive and aggressive focus points, and that the assaults must be militarily and morally humiliating and decisive. Che saw the absurdly lonely figure of David, standing up to Goliath, as an essential factor in David's own spiritual rehabilitation.

In the Caribbean, Latin America and elsewhere throughout the dispossessed world (and this does not exclude certain bruised and declining developed countries), Che believed in liberation at any price for the exploited and dominated, and his Cuban and Bolivian call has been that the dynamic movements of the people in the under-developed sectors will create their new leaders who will be avenging and revolutionary; Che was not without the fervour of idealism, tempered as it was with sound, international political good sense.

What does all this mean to me? What did Che's life and death mean in plain, human terms? Each was a lesson in living; each was a definition towards the fuller, richer, independent life; each was tragic and beautiful, for me, in the Caribbean, and for me, in Europe and in Asia and Africa. If it is yet possible for those of the revolutionary faith to have hope, may we hope that ' the sad body ' will see us gathered, ' all the men on earth ', and be ' moved ' to leave his death behind and ' walk ' with those of us who need him, and with those who think they do not but who do.

ANDREW SALKEY (Jamaica)

97

Che, where can I write to you? You will tell me where. A miner in Bolivia, a mother in Peru, a guerrilla fighter who may be there now or not, but will be there in the future. I understand all this, Che, because you are the one who taught me and also this letter should not be for you. How can I tell you that I have never cried so much since that night they killed Frank, even though this time I didn't believe it. Everyone was certain, and I said, ' It isn't possible. A bullet can't put an end to what is eternal. You and Fidel have to live on, for if you do not live, how can life go on? In these fourteen years I have seen so many of those I loved dearly die that today I feel weary of life. I feel I have lived too much; the sun is no longer so beautiful; I no longer feel delight when I see the palm tree. At times, like now, though I love life so much that those two things alone make it worth opening my eyes each morning, I wish to have them closed like those others, like you.

How can it be true? This continent does not deserve such a thing. Had your eyes been left open, Latin America would have found her way swiftly. Che, the only thing that could console me is to have gone, too, but I did not go. I am here with Fidel; I have always done what he wished me to do. Do you remember? You promised me in the Sierra; you told me, ' You will not miss coffee, for we shall drink maté.' You had no frontiers, but you promised to call me when you were in your Argentina, and how I waited, since I knew you would make good that promise. Now it cannot be, you were unable, I was unable. Fidel said yes, that it must be true, what sorrow! He could not say ' Che ', so he took hold of himself and said ' Ernesto Guevara.' Thus he told the people, your people. What deep sorrow! I cried for the people, for Fidel, for you, because now I could not go. Later, at the memorial ceremony for you, this great people did not know what honours Fidel would bestow on you. The honour was: artist. I had been thinking that no honour would be great enough; all too trifling; and Fidel, as always, found the true honours: everything you created was perfect, but you created a unique being, you created yourself; you demonstrated how the new man is truly possible. All of us then saw that this new man is a reality, because he exists; you are he. What more can I tell you, Che. If only I knew, like you, how to put things. Anyway, you once wrote me: ' I see you have become a literary person and now master syntax. But I confess to you that the way I like you best is the way you were one New Year's Day, with all the stops out and giving off to beat the band. That image of you and that of the Sierra (even our arguments of those days seem happy memories now) are the ones I keep for my own personal use.' That is why I could never write about you, and I shall always keep the memory.

Ever onward to victory, beloved Che.

HAYDEE SANTAMARIA (Cuba)

You know how much I admire Che Guevara. In fact, I believe that the man was not only an intellectual but also the most complete human being of our age: as a fighter and as a man, as a theoretician who was able to further the cause of revolution by drawing his theories from his personal experience in battle.

JEAN-PAUL SARTRE (France)

Was his death in vain?
The inevitable outcome for a romantic
adventurer whose vision substituted
the impatient clatter of machine gun
bullets for the inevitable unfolding
of the dialectic?

Did he have a chance?

A writer reminds us :

Fidel,
Back in December, 1956, you landed near Niquero
in the Oriente of Cuba with 82 men and a few arms.
Your plan was to ignite an insurrection which would
rid Cuba of Batista in a few *weeks*. Instead, you
were to wander through fields and forests in the
dark, without real food or water, living on sugar
cane for five days and five nights.
In the depth of this disaster, you were to

99

announce to the few men still with you : ' The days of the dictatorship are numbered.'

' This man is crazy,' one of them admits he said to himself.

That man could have been Che.
This is why we will go on.

DANIEL SCHECHTER (USA)

Confused trembling voices will tell us, they are already telling us, that the death of Che Guevara is a useless sacrifice, though a generous one. A desperate act. An explosion, very beautiful but ineffectual, of the romantic revolution. But no — this death is the culmination of a life, of a series of rational decisions. Isn't it rational for a Marxist to plan to transform reality, to change the apparent dark purpose of the world, such as it is and such as is determined by the economic structures and dominant ideologies of imperialism? This death is a political action and it is our duty to clarify and preserve its political significance : its reasons, its causes, its consequences. To learn from this death. To live from this death, fighting.

JORGE SEMPRUN (Spain)

I'm no expert on Guevara, though I have read his book on guerrilla warfare, and many recent articles that have told quite a lot about him — but by no means everything. A great deal is still to come, and poems and plays will be written about him and his life.

Why is this? Guevara was a frail man with certain great and simple ideas. These two qualities made him immortal, and vulnerable. He died young, and to those who killed him he was an outlaw — but a dangerous one. An army was set on him. He carried ideas to Bolivia, a place everyone now says was the wrong one, and I think they are right, but his ideas were never wrong, and his fate was to choose

the wrong place so that his ideas would eventually be proved more right than ever. He was not destined to strike up a spectacular Dien Bien Phu in South America and grow renowned as a general, but what he did do, and leave behind him, will turn out to have been just as vital.

Heroes, theoreticians, martyrs, great leaders will come as they are needed in South America, and Che Guevara had some of all these qualities rolled into his own wide personality.

His ideas were young ideas — they will always be young. In some sense he could not bear to grow old. He didn't have it in him to ' form a government ' — and who can blame him? One must applaud him for wanting to make revolutions rather than governments — which in most cases distort all memory of them, turn them into pageants of inhuman clockwork action.

From the evidence, one can deduce much. He was frail, but had a great idea to sustain his body through immense hardship. Life in the jungle has the most devastating effect on the physical system. To survive a week is to survive a lifetime. But a body can live on ideas, though the man must be of an extreme toughness and be absolutely human at the same time. A fanatic would not survive.

One cannot talk about Guevara, however, as if one knew him at school. Too many, no doubt, now knew him at school for any such evidence to be worth much. But I will stake a lot on certain traits of his character being true, without being tempted into the useless fields of hagiography. In any case, Guevara is no myth. There is someone like him in Colombia at the moment. He is a folk hero though, not only for South America, but for all the world, including the United States. One can easily see why, and if there are any who can't, let them draw their curtains and go back to the fire.

ALAN SILLITOE (England)

Put a bullet in his head
Fields are dumb   the earth is dead
Shoot the rebel from behind
Walls are deaf   the roof is blind
Burn his body   pound his flesh
Blood and water dry to ash

Cut his finger from his hand
Print it as his last command

After Zapata
Lumumba
Nadie y nada

Put a bullet in his head
Fields are marching   earth is red
Shoot the rebel from behind
Walls have ears   the roof a mind
Burn his body   pound his flesh
Blood and water flood the ash
Cut his finger from his hand
Print it as his last command

After Zapata
Lumumba
GUEVARA
Viva la tierra

ANDREW SINCLAIR (England)

Ever since my three-month visit to Cuba in the summer of 1960, the Cuban Revolution has been dear to me, and Che, along with Fidel, have been heroes and cherished models. Che seemed especially compelling. One knew of the intensity of his passion for justice, of his heroic participation in the guerrilla struggle in the Sierra Maestra (in which the usual adversity of struggle was compounded by bouts of crippling asthma), and of the qualities of his mind and the developing maturity of his political thinking as disclosed in his writings and the speeches he delivered between 1959 and 1965. But it was only with his extraordinary letter of April, 1965, to Fidel, renouncing his position in the Cuban government and his Cuban citizenship to participate in revolutionary struggles elsewhere — as we now know, to lead the guerrilla movement in Bolivia — that one began to grasp the full definition that Che had given to the vocation of the revolutionist. ' The duty of every revolutionary is to make the revolution.' Agreed. But what Che demonstrated by his decision of 1965 — which puts everything that he did during his stay in Cuba in a new light, a wider context — is that the revolutionary aspiration must not be enclosed within nationalisms, and ultimately compromised by identification with the interests of separate nation-states.

The shock of Che's death has been tremendous. Apart from a grim sense of the political importance of his loss, I feel a personal grief that will last a long time. Che survives now only in the ' use ' that will be made of his life and his death. What will that use be? I don't disdain the impact of Che as a romantic image, especially among newly radicalised youth in the United States and Western Europe; if the glamour of Che's person, the heroism of his life, the pathos of his death, are useful to young people in strengthening their disaffiliation from the life-style of American imperialism and in advancing the development of a revolutionary consciousness, so much the better. Behind every rhetoric and every struggle stands the figure of an exemplary person. Therefore, it's right that not simply the words and deeds of Che count, but the figure of the whole man. Che is the clearest, most unequivocal image of the *humanity* of the world-wide revolutionary struggle unfolding today. But it is vital not to allow Che, in our memory of him, to become too abstract a figure : the romantic adventurer (like Lord Byron), the noble underdog (like Zapata), the poet-revolutionary (like Martí). What assists in this distortion is, of course, the fact that he has been cut down. Unfortunately, many people find it easier to revere the person of and give assent to the ideas of a revolutionary leader who has been martyred than one who is alive, engaged in struggle, making mistakes, still developing. People find something inherently appealing in Rosa Luxemburg and Karl Liebknecht, in Trotsky, in Abram Leon, Marcel Hic, and Martin Widelin (European Trotskyites killed by the Nazis), in Patrice Lumumba, in Malcolm X, and now in Che. It seems easier to stand with them than with Fidel, with the NLF, with Hugo Blanco in a Peruvian prison, with Stokely and Rap Brown and James Forman. But Che doesn't, because he is dead, become more admirable than Fidel. The trap of sentimentalism must be avoided. Merely to consign Che to the pantheon of martyrs is too easy. It would be, moreover, a profoundly unpolitical response to his death.

Che must not be allowed to become an inspiring ' beautiful ' legend. Far more useful would be to stress his singularity, Che as a *controversial* figure on the contemporary revolutionary scene. Only by paying particular attention to his words and deeds will we do his life and death justice.

107

The main importance of Che is not as a singular personality, a humanly exemplary figure of the 'revolutionary' but as a leader — both in active struggle and theoretical articulation — of a specific movement, the Cuban Revolution, the example of which has revitalized radical consciousness in the 1960's. This in itself has been an enormous contribution and no mean feat, after the lengthy period of cynicism about the validity of Marxist goals induced by the traumatic betrayal of the Russian Revolution by Stalinism and by the counter-revolutionary policies of orthodox communist parties wherever potentially revolutionary situations existed, as in France and Italy in 1945-47 or in Latin America in the last fifteen years (not to mention such outright brutal repressions of democratic revolutionary uprisings, as in Spain in 1936, Poland in 1944, East Germany in 1953, and Hungary in 1956). The behaviour of orthodox, Moscow-oriented communist parties throughout the world since the late 1920's has furnished one of the greatest single obstacles to radical thought and action. But through the example of the new revolutionary options emerging outside of Europe and North America in the neo-colonialist countries, the degenerate revolutionary traditions are finally being effectively contested. It is the independent, though still imperfect and emerging, socialist society of Cuba, along with the heroic struggle of the Vietnamese Revolution which, though it has not yet expelled the American aggressors, has already gone a long way towards expunging its Stalinist heritage, which has given most concrete hope for a revalidation of the Marxist revolutionary tradition.

Che's significance is the role he played in this new revolutionary tradition, which directly opposes major developments in Russia in the last thirty years, in the European states since World War II, and in China. For the revolutionary tradition is not something that can be adhered to *en bloc*. The painful lesson that has been learned is that conformist, anti-democratic, and counter-revolutionary movements can and have used revolutionary theory as mere 'ideology', to promote the interests of a given nation-state (either as a bureaucratic élite exercising power within a nominally 'socialist' country, or as a legitimate minority party effectively supporting the status quo in capitalist or neo-colonial countries). Che more than once quoted Lenin's dictum, 'Without a revolutionary theory there is no revolutionary practice.' True enough. But without an effective, active recognition of the *internationalism* of authentic revolutionary struggle and a genuine substantive commitment to *democratic* practices, any revolutionary movement or party must decay into a new vehicle of political oppression and buttress a reconstituted class society. Upon these two principles, Che formed the core of his revolutionary theory. On the internationalism of the revolutionary movement he staked his own life, by the exemplary didactic act of leaving Cuba to engage in struggle in Bolivia. And Che's role in promoting the creation of socialist democracy in Cuba is less well known, but equally important. It was Che, for instance, who dissuaded Fidel early in 1959, after the revolution took power, from disarming the guerrilla movement and forming a regular army; and argued, successfully, for the creation of a nation-wide militia which would entail that the entire populace continue to bear arms. It is Che who is mainly responsible for the liberty for all tendencies in the arts, including thoroughly apolitical and avant-garde ones, which exists in Cuba. This is hardly to say that the Cuban society has completely achieved the aims of socialist democracy and justice; in at least two important respects, the absence of a free press and of an independent judiciary, it has not. Nevertheless, despite these defects and others, Cuba is in some respects the most genuinely democratic country in the world today; and that is in great measure due to Che's leadership. The fact that Cuba is not still further along the road towards socialist democracy may be partly because Che devoted more and more of his attention and leadership to the first question, that of the internationalism of revolutionary struggle.

Che's argument was that the Revolution in Cuba is not worth preserving, indeed it cannot be preserved *as a humane democratic socialism,* unless it is extended. This is why the Cuban leadership has staked its existence on the spread of revolution to the rest of Latin America. (We know that this argument, eloquently sponsored by Che, was vigorously opposed by the old-line communist party leadership; and that this leadership, under the title of the 'micro-faction' of Annibal Escalante, was brought to trial and condemned quite recently, shortly after the betrayal and death of Che.) This small, precariously located country of six million people could easily have settled for a status quo nationalist 'communism' like Yugoslavia, that threatened nobody — keeping peace with the Soviet Union and arranging an eventual limited accommodation with the United States. Instead, Cuba has chosen to defy not only the United States with its blockade, its constant threat of invasion, but also to defy Russia, on which it is dependent for economic support, and to dispute with China as well.

This policy, of which Che is reported to be the principal architect, should not altogether surprise us. In its incredible idealism and daring, it is exactly commensurate with the grandiose task which the Cuban Revolution has set itself. In his essay on *Man and Socialism in Cuba,* written in 1965 for a radical magazine in Uruguay while he was travelling in Africa, Che reaffirmed the classical Marxist horizon of socialist revolution — nothing less than the creation of a new man.

> ' It is the 21st century man we must create, although this is still a subjective and not a realised aspiration. It is precisely this man of the next century who is one of the fundamental objectives of our work. . . .'

Che himself was not, could not be that new man. But what gives his life its ultimate moral authority is his commitment to that goal, which is nothing less than the cause of humanity itself.

SUSAN SONTAG (USA)

TUNE FOR CHE

Che, your comrades will create
A hymn from you of love and hate

Your body is their instrument
Of faith and courage and dissent

Keys have been made from all your bones
To play the scale of human groans

Your skin is stretched to make a drum
That plays the beat of fights to come

From your throat they've made a flute
That pleads for those who are still mute

From your lips a whistle calls
Every time a just man falls

Your heart's a bell that rings each time
An unjust man commits a crime

A guitar from your rib-cage
Plays the sorrow of our age

Your sinews have become the strings
That weep each time the guitar sings

Each of your words is now a song
Which has the power to right a wrong

Each deed a note, each note a word
Each word a song that can be heard

And the foe learns to his cost
That nothing of you has been lost

Do you see, Che, what love can do
For those you loved who now love you?

B. STEPHENS (USA)

Che was the first continental and international Latin American revolutionary that I knew in Cuba. On May 1st, 1964, during a pause in the public holiday, body present and heart faraway, that's how I saw him, solitary in the shade of the statue of Martí, smoking and reading in the smoke some vision, faraway from where or when, travelling through history. I took his photograph and he went on smiling his grave smile, the violent patience of the faraway look in his eyes looking into the future. We were introduced, we had a small coffee, and that was all.

I told my Italian friends in Cuba and afterwards my Cuban friends in Italy : ' I could swear that Che is a poet, and I never make a mistake in my intuitions; Che writes poetry. . . .' They laughed in my face. Miguel Barnet answered that his poetry was action, the pistol was his pen. But I was not convinced because Che was a complete man, and he wrote with pen and pistol, with thought as well as action, with words and mind. He was a human message and wrote messages to be read, which must be read with great attention : A complete man with a message that will print itself on the hard face of the earth.

GIANNI TOTI (Italy)

His revolutionary practice confirms the knowledge of reality and not of scholastic masters. He is a conscientious revolutionary, not a dreamer nor a rebel, and still less an adventurer in the narrow sense; although, on the other hand, all revolutions like all true creations have something of the uncertain and something of the unpredictable, and, therefore, of adventure. If, then, what defines the true revolutionary of our times — the Marxist Leninist — is the narrow bond between theory and practice, between the thought and the action, Che is of that breed, of those rising as much over utopian dreams as over empiricism. They fight according to a plan that grows and is nourished by the proper reality. For that reason nobody like him emphasized in those days the role of one's conscience, or more exactly, the role of conscientious action not only in the revolutionary process but also in the construction of the new society. El Che, for that reason, has been a faithful exponent of a political revolutionary reality which has nothing to do with idealistic romanticism nor with the dangerous reality which degenerates into opportunism or into politics without principles.

Che has fought and has fallen in the most hard and difficult conditions. His death came not as a result of an implacable necessity nor of a tragic battle, desperate and without escape; but as a real possibility on which he counted at any given moment, and which he must have looked coldly in the face. His death is terribly painful. From it, his example makes sense. He is the revolutionary leader who, after measuring conscientiously the historical possibilities, contributed to their desperate actions. It is the death of a revolutionary who dies conscious that history is not written in a single day or in a few weeks, but in a long process which determined fighting helps to shorten. In this process victories and defeats alternate until the final victory.

The lesson of the life and death of Che confirms, once again, that history is made by real men, and that the revolution can only be brought about by those who raise themselves from the condition of mere products of a social structure to men conscious of history. And that is why, on this ground, Che's words and actions, his life and death, bore perfect witness to what man can do in our time, when he is filled with a true socialist conscience. For that reason, Che is inconceivable without socialism. But in turn, the socialism of Marx and Lenin is inconceivable without Che.

ADOLFO SANCHEZ VAZQUEZ (Mexico)

It is three years since I was in Brazil. I saw the misery in the north-west, the peasants grown stupid without even the strength to complain or hate.

Their material conditions have not improved, but for some years since the Cuban Revolution, men like Guevara have been with them. They rouse them and light a fuse of resistance, a revolutionary conscience; they make a decision against all hypocritical reform, disguised as an impossible coexistence with imperialism.

Whoever has been in those lands is conscious that there is no middle of the road. Actions and men seen from Europe can appear irrational, the stuff of historical legend, of courage without end. Yet in South America, these actions and war are the only positive forces, precisely rational for their extreme impetus and total subversion.

In these days, we can say in one breath : Latin America, Cuba, Vietnam — Guevara :

The lesson we learn from him : a total coherence, an extreme force of conscience to fight imperialism, no matter where it may be.

EMILIO VEDOVA (Italy)

He died just when we needed him
More than ever before.
Why did he die?
Was he sick? Had he lost faith?
Was it perhaps a sacrifice?
But if he was sick, why didn't we help him?
He was like a Christ taken down from the Cross . . .
I loathe the heroics of pain
I loathe the mystique of resurrection
We abandoned him
When we ought to have helped him with all our might.
The very earth which drank his blood was not his earth;
Only the land where you live is yours.
And now we're turning him into a martyr
To ease our own consciences.
Or am I making a mistake?
Was he perhaps strong and active and full of faith?

Was he perhaps the only one who *dared*?
Did his death teach us our cowardice?
Learn
Learn
Learn
The struggle continues.

PETER WEISS (Germany)

What can I say to you, Che Guevara?
Only that I feel sorrow
Because I did not know you better.
And shame
Because I did so little to help.

I am fifty years of age, Che Guevara,
I will not bother to describe myself
I am sure you get the picture.
Even a super-silver stainless blade
Cannot shave away
The grey hostages I have given
To expediency.
The comfortable compromising
And the flatulent phrases.
Such as
' The need to be patient '
And ' to exercise restraint '
The suggestion that Socialism
' Is, perhaps, an old-fashioned notion,
Rendered obsolete by modern technology '
Or that
' Freedom, after all,
Is a relative concept '
Above all,
That ' the hero has no place
In Literature.
Or in Life, for that matter '

You were a real and actual man, Che Guevara
In your dying

114

There was no myth
No trick to fool the simple.
Your body did not arise on the Third Day.
In practical terms
You are quite dead.

But you have proved to me, Che Guevara
That all the vinegar years
Have not entirely soured the wine of youth.
Freedom,
Is still more than just a word to me.

What do you mean to me, Che Guevara?
Of course, you were a hero.
But I think of you as a friend
As a good comrade
Who is still with us.

Of course, your name will be honoured.
My children and their children
Shall say it as easily
As if it were their own.
But more important than all this
I shall try
A little harder
Because of you
To climb the forbidding and inhospitable mountain.

TED WILLIS (England)

' Whether he now rests in an anonymous grave, or whether he has, once again, escaped to re-appear elsewhere, this courageous man deserves both respect and honour.' The author of these lines is an American, writing an editorial in the *New York Times*. The man he is describing is, of course, Che Guevara, enemy number one of the United States.

I met him only once, in 1960, in the early days of the Cuban Revolution. He was president of the Bank of Cuba then. On an impulse, I had sent him a telegram from the African capital where I was staying. Two days later, I received an answer: Comandante

Ernesto Guevara will see you on Tuesday at noon.

At the appointed time, I was in Havana, in the waiting room of the Bank of Cuba. Two or three minutes later, the door of the lift opened and a very young, square-shouldered man with an extremely pale face strode into the room. As he came over to shake hands with me, I neither noticed his straggly beard nor his blue-black beret with its red star. I saw only his large black eyes which smiled when his lips smiled. I had expected to meet a hard man, and instead there stood before me an almost timid man in whom gentleness was the key-note.

We spoke for three and a half hours and our conversation made a profound impact on me. Guevara was not like any of the other outstanding men I have met before or since. A lot has been said about his romanticism, his poetry; a lot has also been said about his revolutionary intransigeance. Yet he was too precise, too organised, to be a poet or a romantic; and the man who wrote, ' I must say, even at the risk of seeming ridiculous, that the true revolutionary is guided by motives of love,' cannot be that professional advocate of violent revolution that some have made him out to be.

The man who, at the age of twenty-four, abandons his country, his studies, his family and his middle-class standard of living to set off on a bicycle towards the unknown; the man who, at that age, has already gone beyond the narrow confines of patriotism to join the struggle against injustice in Guatemala, then Mexico, then Cuba; the man who, twelve years later, with the final outcome of the revolution he helped bring about still in balance, leaves it in the hands of his companions-in-arms and sets off again, writing to Fidel: ' Other nations in the world call for my modest efforts. . . . That if my final hour comes beneath other skies, my last thought will be for this people and especially for you. . . . That I leave my wife and my children nothing, and I am not sorry, but glad it should be so. That I can do nothing for them as the State will give them enough to live on and will educate them . . .' that man has no equal in the world today. He reconciles the most pessimistic to the human race. I feel proud that he was a citizen of the Third World.

Like all great men, he knew he was different from the others, more sensitive, more complete. What distinguished him from the other great men and that he had in common with Lenin, was that it never was a source of vanity for him and that he never felt the least contempt for others. On the contrary, he would have wanted all men to feel as he did; at most, he sometimes felt irritated or dis-

116

tressed that they did not. The one idea which obsessed him all his life was: to transform the alienated man of today into the new liberated man of tomorrow. 'Each individual would feel inwardly richer and more responsible within himself. The vital thing is for men to become more conscious each day of the need to incorporate themselves within their society and at the same time to realise their own significance within that society.'

'The road is long and some of it is unmapped. We will often have to turn back, and at times we will find that we have gone too fast and left the masses behind. At other times, because we will have gone too slowly, we will feel the masses pressing at our heels. As revolutionaries, we try to go as quickly as possible, clearing the way, but we know that we have to rely on the masses and that they will advance rapidly only if they have our example to follow.'

The man who wrote these lines, who did what Guevara has done, and who lived his life, deserves the respect of everyone, including those to whom his name was anathema.

If he is dead, as we are told he is, he died fighting in the service of the idea which never left him, with the certainty that he had: 'worked to consolidate the revolution honourably and with enough devotion.' Let us only hope that, in the last instants of his life, he kept all his faith.

BECHIR BEN YAHMED (Tunisia)

LIST OF PLATES

103   *Top:* Two photographs of Che Guevara in Bolivia where he was leader of a guerrilla band until his death in October, 1967.
Bottom: Fidel Castro announcing to the people of Cuba on October 10th, 1967, that he is convinced that the murdered guerrilla leader known as Ramón is in fact Che Guevara.

104   *Top:* Bolivian officers, soldiers and journalists in the town of Vallegrande, inspecting the dead body of Che Guevara.
Bottom: Close-up of the dead leader's face. A photograph of him alive has been placed next to him for identification.

INDEX

119